THOSE DARN STRIPES

To Dad

I tried my best to recreate events, locations and conversations from my memories of them. In order to protect people's privacy, in some instances I have changed the names of individuals and places, some identifying characteristics and details such as physical features, occupations and places of residence.

CONTENTS

We spend so much time in our lives dwelling on our weaknesses and faults; wishing to be things we are not and can never be for they are not our nature. A rabbit cannot be a bear no matter how hard it strives! A zebra could be a horse; if not for those darn stripes! Turtles don't run fast and horses only fly in myth. Find out what you are and be satisfied with it! We are not all things, but we are all something. Walk in the light, have a kind and empathetic soul. Be what you are, for all things are beautiful when honestly displayed.

—Jay W. Nelson (my father)

Not a Plain Jay

A Tough Guy

A few summers ago, Jay and I went on a canoe trip. We were less than ten minutes into our voyage down the river when our canoe capsized. When I oriented myself, I stood up in the waist-deep river and noticed the canoe was slowly drifting away … upside down. I caught up to the canoe and tried to tip it right-side-up, but the weight of the water that the craft had swallowed made this task nearly impossible … so I thought. From out of nowhere, Jay shoved me aside and focused on the canoe. With both hands, Jay grabbed the canoe by one of its long edges, pulled it above his waist and held it seemingly effortlessly until all the water drained out.

"What a tough guy," I thought to myself.

Jay proudly stands 5 feet, 9 inches tall. He has a barrel chest and shoulders that could carry a house. His Popeye-like forearms and thickly callused hands give proof of 25 years in the construction industry. (Most smokers use trays for their cigarettes; Jay simply cups his free hand to catch the fallen ashes.) Heavily scarred and overtaken by protruding veins, Jay's arms look like they are on the brink of eruption. Although his graying hair and full beard provide little evidence of the light brown color they once were, Jay's piercing blue eyes are still full of youth. Behind his prized facial hair lies a rugged, weather-beaten face showing the wear and tear of a hard life. Jay's thin waist sits below a taut abdomen while his skinny legs contradict his upper bod.

According to Ron, one of Jay's coworkers, "he's fifty and in better shape than the rest of us [the other men in the company] combined." (Most of his fellow ironworkers are in their twenties and thirties.)

To match his powerful figure, Jay has a low, booming voice that is perfect for an ironworker foreman. Whether his men are 50 or 500 feet away from him, the sound of his orders resonates through their ears. ("Hurry up … you're a dime holding up a dollar! Are you trying to piss me off? Hey guys, let's get the hell outta here.") Even with nearby traffic, the hollers of other men, or the sounds of heavy machinery cannot drown out the sound of Jay's voice on the job.

Jay has a strut that, upon first sight, made a friend say, "What a hard-ass." It is as if he is walking in slow motion while listening to hard rock music. He takes long, powerful strides that almost seem too long for his legs. To match his steps, Jay swings his arms at the same slow pace with his fists half open, on the verge of being clenched. The emotionless expression on Jay's face is diluted by the determination in his transfixed pupils. In fact, his strut is so recognizable that it spans decades.

Last summer, Jay was walking back to his house after checking the mailbox down the street. Before he reached the front steps, a car pulled up to the end of his driveway with its driver leaning out of the window.

"Jay!" he yelled.

Jay turned around and slowly approached the stranger in the vehicle. It was Dave, one of his Marine Corps buddies. Dave had gained a significant amount of weight, which explained why Jay did not recognize him right away.

On the other hand, it was much easier for Dave to notice Jay.

"I recognized you by your walk," Dave said, even though the last time these men had seen each other was in 1975.

An Unchangeable Man

One morning, I stopped by Jay's house to see if he wanted to ride to work together. Jay, who enjoys driving alone, hesitantly accepted. Obviously frustrated because I disrupted his usual morning procedure, Jay quietly transferred his tool belt from his car to mine. Before he got into my truck, Jay looked at me disgustingly and said, "It is hard to change an unchangeable man." An "unchangeable man" is the perfect phrase to describe him. In many ways, you can set your watch to Jay.

Every morning before work, Jay wakes up around four. He then goes to the kitchen and turns on the radio, which is always set on WCCO, his favorite AM station. For the next two hours, Jay sits at the kitchen table, has a couple cups of instant coffee and smokes a few KOOLs. (They have to be this brand; Jay has smoked them since he was 17 years old.) Often, he will hum songs from his youth, such as Gene Pitney ditties, as he listens to the traffic updates and weather reports given every eight minutes by the radio announcers. Sometimes

Jay sings these songs aloud to a loyal audience — the calico, orange, and gray cats that take turns rubbing up against his shins. He responds to their meows by addressing them as if they are his newborn children while rubbing his hands across the fur on their heads and backs. He leaves the room every once in a while, to get dressed or go to the bathroom, but always returns to the kitchen. About twenty minutes before he leaves, Jay goes outside to start his car, which is parked on the street in front of the house. It is a rusty, red 1987 Honda Prelude that takes a long time to warm up in the cool Minnesota mornings. Adorned in a worn-out hooded sweatshirt, faded jeans, and brown work boots, he makes sure the cats have food and water, turns off the kitchen light, and is out the door.

During the workday, Jays does not eat.

For breakfast? Coffee and cigarettes.

For lunch? Coffee and cigarettes.

After work, Jay's diet comprises a smorgasbord of desserts, making up for his lack of nutrients during the day. He eats chocolate ice cream by the bowlful and candy bars by the score. Jay is partial to chocolate. Chocolate-covered donuts and cookies, not to mention semi-sweet treats containing coconut or peanuts, are among his favorites. If not eating desserts, he usually consumes beef of chicken pot pies, cocktail weenies and cooked pork by the can, fried hamburgers, or fish sticks. Still, Jay does not forget to incorporate a steady intake of coffee and cigarettes during his nighttime feast.

On the weekends, it is a daylong binge. Coffee, cigarettes, and a plethora of the foods he usually eats at night.

Although he has had a beard for the last quarter-century, Jay is a chameleon of sorts. Because he has to work outside, Jay grows his hair according to the weather.

In the winter, he looks like a lumberjack. Jay's hair gets very long and wavy while his wild beard practically covers his face, similar to Grizzly Adams. He says it keeps his face warm, and no one denies it. Often in the dead of winter, Jay is the only one on the job site who does not have his face or ears covered by a cap or mask.

In the summer, Jay gets a crew cut because long hair is "a pain in the ass."

After his first haircut of the year, the guys at work usually have to do a double-take because they do not recognize him without his long locks.

"It takes years off him," his fellow ironworkers have said.

During the warmer months, Jay also keeps his beard groomed and trimmed so neatly that it looks like gray carpet. But he will never shave the whole thing off. Jay keeps his beard "to hide [his] ugly face" or because he doesn't "want to shave every f---in' day."

The more people tell Jay to do something, the more he won't just to spite them. If you tell him that smoking is bad (he smokes between two and three packs a day) and that he should quit, Jay will probably say, "I know", light a cigarette, and blow the smoke in your face. Or, he will simply come to terms with his own mortality by saying, "Why? I'm gonna die, anyway."

Jay does not like doctors. The last place on Earth he would be is the doctor's office. A few years ago, Jay fell ten feet off a wall he was constructing, landed in a pile of rubble, and severely sprained his right ankle. After seeing that Jay could barely walk, his son suggested that he go to the doctor.

"Why?" Jay responded. "They are already going to tell me s--- I already know."

He hobbled to work the very next day with his right ankle twice the size of his left.

The last time Jay actually went to the doctor, he was told that he needed knee surgery. That was well over a year ago, and he has not been back since. Despite the unrelenting pain in his knee, Jay still refuses to undergo surgery. The man would much rather be on his deathbed than a hospital bed.

You Think You Know Him, But…

Despite his tough-guy image, the few people who do know Jay find him to be quite pleasant. His childlike sense of humor sits well with his coworkers. Jay can often be heard singing classic rock songs aloud at work with slight modifications. He changes the lyrics to include the names of men on the job site.

Or, Jay sings insulting phrases in a positive tone, such as "Oh, I hate Dusty [a young coworker] … yes I do!"

Jay is genuine and has never been afraid to tell someone how he truly feels. He once told a librarian to "stick [her] policy up [her] ass" when his son, who forgot his library card, was denied access to a computer. His son found it humorous, but it appalled the librarian and several other people in the lobby.

Whether it is a pauper or the Pope, his reaction would be the same. He does not believe in changing his ways for anyone. A few years ago, Jay told an incompetent job superintendent to "get f---ed" and walked off the site. Although he was the foreman, Jay didn't come back until the following week, leaving his men in limbo during his absence.

"He was PISSED!" exclaimed Troy, a former coworker.

Jay's nothing-to-hide attitude may rub some the wrong way, but it commands an enormous amount of respect for those that are familiar with him.

"I like him because what you see is what you get," said Mindy, an old friend of Jay's.

The man who sometimes yells at the television as if it were the bane of his existence also falls asleep to the likes of Steinbeck, Thoreau, Emerson, and Dafoe. The man who could write a dictionary of expletives to use at work also quotes Shakespeare and Longfellow; has a wealth of knowledge concerning current events and history; and is an excellent tutor for his college-aged sons. And the man whose 22-year marriage ended in a bitter divorce a few years ago does not let a day go by without making sure his struggling ex-wife is doing ok.

"He has a big heart," says Beth, his former spouse.

Unfortunately, most people do not get to see this side of him. Jay is a seclusive man who doesn't leave his house unless he has to go to work, cash his paycheck, buy groceries, or take an occasional trip to the casino. He has never needed or wanted recognition, nor have the opinions of others ever mattered to him. According to Jay, he wants nothing more than his "fair share." The thing that is important to him is the wellbeing of his family. This drives Jay through every day; nothing hurts him more than seeing his sons unhappy.

A few months ago, Jay left his stressed-out son a note that characterized his compassion.

"Ease up on yourself and appreciate those who love you," he wrote.

Appreciate Those Who Love You…

After reading this, I thought about all the baseball games he never missed, the breakfasts we have talked over, and the phone calls I received when he had not heard from me in a day or two. I remembered all the "I'm very proud of you[s]", the "drive safely[s]", and the "I love you[s]." And I recalled how, not too long ago, he told me to move home, built a room for me, and, despite lacking a college education, convinced me to stay in school. He believed in me when I didn't believe in myself.

I also wondered about children with abusive fathers, with deadbeat dads, or who have no fathers at all. I was reminded of my friends who never saw their dads—or who didn't want to see their fathers—and realized how lucky I was.

"Have you ever wondered how you ended up with such a cool dad?" he often asks me in a joking manner.

I usually respond with a laugh, but he's right.

If I have children someday, I only hope that I can love them as much as Jay Nelson has loved me.

This story originally appeared in the July/August 2003 edition of The Ironworker.

Introduction

It took me a while to get out of bed each day. A heavy heart anchored me to my mattress, killing my desire to attack mornings like I used to. Besides, I lay as long as possible to compensate for the previous night. The anguish of a recent tragedy weighed on my mind, causing me to toss and turn through the wee hours without fail. I eventually fell asleep as dawn neared, but it was never enough. The sound of garages opening, autos starting, and car stalls closing usually woke me up soon after. I studied the ceiling till the sunlight seeping around the blinds got annoying or my caffeine headache made itself known; whichever came first.

Promptly pouring myself a cup of Joe, I normally sprawled out anew — on the living room couch this round — to occupy my brain with thoughtless TV. I nonetheless changed my routine a few weeks ago. Instead of watching the same sports highlights hour after hour, I began wandering into my office. I figured it was about time to be somewhat productive, aim for something more than simply exist. I also desperately needed an outlet to help me battle the depression that had taken over my soul.

Searching my laptop, I revisited many stories — an unfinished collection of narratives — I had written prior to my abrupt halt six moons before. I read them in chronological order. And after scrolling through the pieces, I realized the rollercoaster of emotions I had ridden over the course of these accounts. It bothered me, though, that I had not yet expressed some of my rawest moods. My original intention with this project was to reveal more of myself, and I believed that if I was going to do so, I had to show all of my stripes, whether they were pleasing, embarrassing, or just plain ugly. So I wrote again. Not only did I have pent-up feelings to release, but I wanted to depict some significant people and places in my life as well. It was the perfect task to throw my anxious self into.

 This book shares images from the past thirty-one months of a 31-year-old, who's still trying to sort things out. But most important, it symbolizes the way I finally began coping with the toughest hardship I've ever encountered.

Bass Ponds, Bloomington, Minnesota

1

Bass Ponds

I hadn't been here in forever. The biting wind made my eyes water and nose run as I watched my breath drift away and disappear into the morning air. A familiar sensation came over me while I tuned in to dead leaves dancing atop the asphalt. It was definitely November in Minnesota.

Suddenly, I recognized something else. Slowly approaching me from the other side of the empty lot was that same old Chevy Cavalier, same old tree-shaped freshener dangling from the rearview, and the same old blue eyes piercing through the windshield. The white auto rolled past me and parked next to my black Ford Ranger.

"Well, if it isn't my son … and his better-looking dad!" the graying man exclaimed while getting out of the car, grinning behind his wild beard.

"Hey Pop!" I replied, sporting a smile larger than his.

"Been a while since we've been here," he added.

"Yeah, but it's good to be back. I've always liked this place."

After dodging a few of his jabs (he enjoys pretending to box), I followed my father, and we gradually descended the sloped entrance into Bloomington's Bass Ponds.

It didn't take long before I concluded that nothing had changed. Ducks still lazily floated on the calm waters, the dam beavers continued to leave a path of destruction (clear by countless fallen or half-eaten trunks on the verge of collapsing), and the surrounding branches donned striking yellow, green, and auburn hues like they invariably had during this season.

As I meandered amongst the scenery, I took a walk down memory lane, too. I reflected upon yesteryear and envisioned a much younger version of me. I saw myself stepping on the same gravelly tracks, standing no taller than my dad's bellybutton, and frequently stopping with him to view various birds fly overhead, turtles sunbathe on logs, and the occasional deer that crossed our path. I chuckled when I thought about my pop's keen eye. We would spend hours upon hours scanning the wilderness because of his genuine appreciation of nature. He never rushed because he didn't want to miss anything—a trait I've truly admired.

Returning to the present, I noted that my father hadn't lost his sixth sense. He routinely spun around to rustles I couldn't hear and would squint deep into the woods. I paused whenever he did, looking and listening intently to the things he pointed out. More often than not, he would show me an animal staring back at us with its beady eyes or a critter I almost stepped on. But I didn't come to the Bass Ponds just to study the outdoors.

Aside from helping me spot wildlife, Jay Nelson has guided me in additional ways. He's listened without fail, provided me with invaluable advice, and has usually steered me in the right direction. On this day, he was giving his unsettled, unemployed son a much-needed confidence boost.

"Ease up on yourself. You've got a lot to be proud of. I know *I'm* proud of you," he said while slapping me on the back. "Something good will happen if you just hang in there."

We kept walking and talking, exploring all the woodland trails. And after hearing my pop's reassurances throughout the morn, I could somehow see the forest instead of the trees. I no longer felt worthless because I didn't have a job.

It was midday when we began the hike back to our vehicles. The uphill climb was quite a struggle when I was little; I used to lag way behind my towering dad. I shook my head in disbelief when I realized how time had flown. Now, we were virtually the same size, and I walked alongside him as we left the Bass Ponds, stride for stride.

I also realized that although we stood shoulder to shoulder, I still looked up to my father. And I always will.

2

The Power of Ten

The number ten stands out to me. It represents the amount of days I was a proud member of a Global Village team. On behalf of Twin Cities Habitat for Humanity, my seventeen teammates and I left the biting Minnesota January for the sweltering heat of Puerto Ángel, Mexico—a fishing hamlet on the Pacific. We excitedly absorbed our host culture, witnessed magnificent sites, and met fascinating people during our week and a half in the tranquil pueblo. But what I recall most is digging trenches, mixing cement, and tying rebar under 90-plus temps and hellacious humidity. My colleagues and I actually spent most of our stint working alongside area residents to build the foundation of a home for a household in need. It was an extremely gratifying trip; ten *días* I will always remember.

The number ten is also meaningful to Marcelo, the lively homebuyer whose house we worked on. A former soccer prodigy himself, "Maca" has the utmost respect for the digits worn by Pelé and Maradona—a pair of the game's legends. The exuberant 22-year-old actually dons the *diez* while starring for Pollería Dagmar; one of a dozen squads that battle on weekday afternoons. However, despite Marcelo's love of the sport, ten means much more to him outside of *fútbol*. Habitat for Humanity Oaxaca has shown him the actual power of ten.

The design of the local affiliate is unique because it requires a tensome of households to construct ten casas. This scheme creates a strong sense of community; given that homebuyers have to continue their sweat equity until they complete all ten dwellings. In fact, the tenth house must be finished before program participants can move into their new abodes. Since the families look out for each other while their houses are going up, they will probably do the same long after they lay the last brick.

Marcelo was still living with his spouse, Rosalena, and two young boys, Emanuel and Marcel, under his parents' roof. He wanted some privacy, his own place for the *familia* he had started, but just couldn't make ends meet selling bottled water in the streets of Puerto Ángel. So he seriously considered moving to the United States several months ago. He wished to find a higher-paying job in order to better support his wife and children. Maca desired to remain with his loved ones in Mexico, and, fortunately, was accepted into Habitat Oaxaca's program shortly thereafter. Not only was he relieved that he didn't have to leave, but he knew his family would soon be part of a much bigger one as well.

And after our crew's time with Marcelo, we felt like his family was part of ours, too.

Workday #1, Puerto Ángel, Oaxaca, México

3

Peering off the Pier

I continued to sweat while the sun set over the coast of southern Mexico. Although night was near, the sweltering heat refused to leave with the disappearing daylight. Yet I was fine. The cool Pacific waves washing my toes were rather refreshing. The breathtaking beach ahead took my mind off the high temps as I wandered toward the Oaxacan afterglow.

Slowly walking Playa Principal, Puerto Ángel's bay captivated me. I ogled the pacifying palms that skirted the golden dunes. I gazed at the bright white fishing vessels, which flaunted striking blue interiors, neatly parked on the shore. And I was speechless because of the hush of the harbor. Aside from the faint laughter of children playing in the water, the only noise I heard was the great gusts of wind sweeping across my face. I sometimes felt like I was in a sandy sound chamber while I explored the pleasant port.

I kept to the oceanfront and ultimately reached the landing that jutted far beyond the eastern shallows. Unimpressed by the weathered wharf, I spun and noticed something which immediately caused me to forget about the ugly concrete at my feet. Just above the tops of the trees stood a tiny, Easter-colored chapel. The kirk gave off a fun and inviting vibe. Its funky appearance and excellent view of the Bahía de Puerto Ángel tempted me to peek at its pews. However, I glimpsed at the rapidly darkening skies and knew I had no choice but to postpone my visit. A trek to the holy house would have to be tomorrow's adventure.

Turning my back on the church, I focused on the end of the pier.

Patiently making my way to its edge, I often stopped to avoid stray dogs, swooping gulls, and kids chasing each other. I further paused to say hello to those also out for an evening stroll. I finally arrived at my destination as the remaining handful of anglers carefully angled around the dock, deposited their crafts on the bank, and carried the day's catch into town.

It was dusk, and I stared in awe, gawking at the lonely boats resting atop the waves while the sol fell behind the cove's cliffs. The closing rays warmly lit the calming waters, and the silence was stronger than ever. The beauty and stillness of nightfall left me with a powerfully peaceful sensation. I couldn't remember the last moment I had witnessed a scene so relaxing.

With the sun now gone until dawn, I decided I should go as well. I started retracing my steps to the hotel and realized I had no idea of the time. Curious, I glanced at my right wrist and saw nothing—I had left my watch in my room.

But I didn't glower over the hour in the long run. I was in no hurry. If anything, I wished I could have rewound the clock to peer off that pier just a little more.

Playa Principal, Puerto Ángel, Oaxaca, México

4

Amanda and the Arboretum

It was mid-July. The sky was clear, the sun beamed bright, and the temp felt perfect. The lawns appeared healthy, the vegetation thick and green, and the flowers lured you in with their vibrant colors. Everything seemed to thrive on this picturesque afternoon—everything, that is, but me.

I had checked out. Although I had reached the middle of a gorgeous garden, my mind remained in the car. I couldn't avoid thinking about the missed highway exit, the extra forty minutes of driving, and how, despite my arguing, I knew the delay was my fault. And to make matters worse, the one who justly pointed the finger at me was nowhere to be found. There I stood, surrounded by breathtaking scenery, and I couldn't care less.

A familiar sound snapped me out of my…

"There you are! What the heck is taking you so long?! You are sure moving slow for someone who was in such a hurry to get here!" yelled the blonde spitfire, rapidly approaching me on the cement path. "It's pointless … we should've stayed home … we're not gonna have enough time…" Amanda went on, impressively lowering her voice to do her best imitation of me.

I simply chuckled and shook my head. I didn't know how else to respond. She was right, and I loved how she never hesitated to put me in my place. It was that spunk which had attracted me to her so many years earlier.

"Sorry," I muttered.

"You're too much. Did you get any nice shots?"

"No, not yet."

Minnesota Landscape Arboretum, Chaska

"Well, good thing you brought *that.*"

I promptly grabbed for the strap slung over my shoulder, removed the Canon from its case and turned it on. Besides enjoying rare free time with my girlfriend, snapping photographs was the reason I wanted to visit the Minnesota Landscape Arboretum.

Before this day trip, the photographer in me was freaking out. I hadn't taken pictures in months. So with camera in hand, I eagerly followed Amanda into the umpteen gardens ahead.

We wandered into the Terrace Garden, which mixed purple and yellow blooms. We admired lots of dwarf conifers, endless evergreens that lined our lane. Schlepping through the Perennial Garden, my girl and I pored over the cobalt water of a central pool hedged with gray and blue frondescence. We skirted an area flaunting pink peonies, orange lilies, and scarlet daylilies. We strolled along a walk bordered with myriad stunning roses, and I frequently stopped to appreciate their fresh linen scent. This pretty promenade brought us to the Japanese Garden, which not only relaxed us with its tiny waterfall but also impressed us with its intricately detailed granite lanterns. We headed toward a glade that showed off azure-leaved hostas, ferns, and shade-loving perennials. Prior to visiting the Woodland Azalea Garden, we studied a fruit and vegetable patch. We sat for a few minutes, scanning the glossy jade foliage of the surrounding hollies. And just when Amanda and I thought we had seen it all, we discovered that the walking paths we had traversed led to additional walking paths; twelve miles of hiking courses actually snaked across this thousand-acre oasis. We locked eyes, recognizing there were many more strides to take. We were game.

Barely on the second part of our tour, Amanda and I realized the vastness of the arboretum. Forests awaited us in all directions. We tackled the trails, passing countless maples, oaks, pines, crabapple and nut trees. We ambled around twenty acres of restored prairie, ogled a wetland sedge meadow, and circled various lochs—one being the home of a constructed Nessie, which creepily bobbed up and down in mucky water.

The afternoon culminated in the Maze Garden. In fact, there were two mazes on the enormous lawn. The neighboring networks rivaled the giant hedge labyrinths seen only behind mansions or in the movies.

Amanda and I first headed for the archway labeled "Adults" and quickly got lost. We tried several routes, but each led to a dead end or other visitors who shared our confusion. Twenty minutes later, we retraced our steps to the entrance, deciding to give the children's labyrinth a go.

This one wasn't any easier. I was wearing down, though the kiddy maze seemed to bring out the child in Amanda. Because my partner was so full of energy, I caught only glimpses of her back.

"C'mon slowpoke!" she once yelled, waving at me from afar.

"Yeah, yeah!" I hollered. I entered the tree-lined tunnel that she was about to leave.

Despite her fast pace, my companion failed to find the outlet as she attacked the puzzle. While I attempted passage after passage, I eventually ran into her somewhere in the labyrinth's heart … I think. And once again, we escaped by shamefully doubling back to the entryway.

To add insult to injury, we soon noticed elated children running out of the exit. But it bothered me just for a minute. Watching my gal's enthusiastic approach to the maze entertained me a lot. She clearly enjoyed herself, so I had fun as well.

Slowly making our way back across the extensive acreage, we not only agreed on the afternoon's disappointments but also spent most of our stroll reliving the highlights. We arrived at our wheels as the sun fell behind the brilliant horizon.

The traffic proved dreadful on the road home. Instead of getting angry, however, my lady popped in one of her favorite CDs and loudly sang along to it. Similar to the manner in which she refused to allow our tense travel to the arboretum ruin her afternoon, she would not let a little gridlock dampen her mood. I laughed during every ditty she vocalized.

That was classic Amanda — always looking to enjoy the ride. And fortunately for me, she was always by my side.

Japanese Garden

5

The Cemetery and Me

The dog days of summer were biting. I sensed the humidity of the mid-August afternoon sinking its teeth into me; the breaths so thick I could almost gnaw them myself. I rolled down my window. I reached across the bench and lowered the other as well. With a five-dollar pair of gas station sunglasses over my eyes, I tilted the sun visor down and let the keys fall into my palm. I started the black pickup, backed out of the driveway, and sped off.

I headed east. Other than that general direction, I had no idea where to roll. But I didn't care. As I shifted into fifth, I tried to drive her out of my skull. The road would be my focus—not her for once. Sweet and endearing one second, pretending I no longer existed the next. And I was an idiot to keep falling for it. Well, not anymore. She had tortured me enough with her mind games. I deserved better. I stepped harder on the accelerator, cranked up the rock tunes, and followed the winding track out of Dodge.

The landscape soon became a blur. I looked ahead, but couldn't see a thing. Blinded by anger, I hated myself for letting my guard down. She got to me when I was weak, offered to be my friend, pretended to listen when I sank into a deep depression, my long relationship at an end. The out-of-the-blue emails, the ceaseless text messages, the marathon calls … all part of some twisted game. When my girlfriend and I separated, I found myself all alone. I rarely saw the deceiver's face. My so-called pal never answered her phone.

These memories caused me to get sick in my stomach. And my foot pushed the gas down farther with each revolting image. I flashed on every occasion I had the chance to tell her to piss off, and each moment she lured me back in. My mobile sat silent for days, but when it buzzed, I foolishly picked up. Her voice always quelled my fury, somehow making me believe she liked me.

St. Patrick Cemetery

So I forgave her again and again. I screamed. The pedal hit the floor.

The tar ahead soon changed into gravel. Dust violently flew up and engulfed the truck, following me like the ominous cloud, the evil woman, who had tailed me for the past few months. Suddenly, the route came to a T. Right or left? Hell, nothing I did lately seemed right. I swung north.

The afternoon wore on, but it wasn't wearing out. It was becoming hotter, in fact. The intense sun baked the two-lane highway; vapor rising like steam coming off a hot mug of coffee. The black pickup doubled as a magnifying glass in this sultry weather. Beads of sweat ran down my forehead, fogging my shades. I chucked them onto the passenger seat. Damn broken air conditioner.

I raced on. I stuck my hand out the window, waving it up and down. The wind rushed up my arm and into my T-shirt, making it puff out. While I enjoyed this refreshing gust, an iron archway caught my eye. Behind it rested a myriad of markers. To the right of the entrance, hanging on a chain-link fence, was a weathered white sign spelling out in charcoal letters: St. Patrick

Inver Grove Heights, Dakota County, Minnesota

Cemetery.

My Ford idled just outside the limits of this city of the dead. I sat there. I wondered why I wanted to go into a graveyard of all places. In that instant, however, it struck me as more like a sanctuary than a bone orchard. These people would actually listen instead of wait to talk. They wouldn't constantly fish for compliments. And they sure as hell wouldn't mock me. I drove in.

Steering onto a small stretch of asphalt, I parked in front of a large utility shed. I exited the Ranger and surveyed the verdant graveyard. Healthy lawns, tall trees, and scattered plots decorated the manicured funerary grounds. The ambiance of the enclosed lot proved much different from the interstate. The noise from the highway had disappeared and a cool breeze blew through the branches, drying my sweat almost immediately. I had goose bumps. An eerie yet peaceful sensation swept over me. I headed for the graves within a stone's throw from my tailgate.

I examined the distinct memorials while touring the tombs. Some sported gigantic crucifixes which stabbed the sky. Others were smaller in stature, sporting shorter crosses. And some were almost hidden because they were miniscule. I risked tripping on them if I overlooked my steps.

The vast majority originated in the early 1900s, and some dated as far back as the 1870s. Yet the well-kept graves still showcased their intricate details. Even the oldest ones looked like they should last for centuries to come.

I also pondered the descent of the individuals beneath the headstones. Who were they? Native Americans? Norwegians? Germans? I began noting the chiseled names. Aside from some newer plots near the entrance, the IDs were all Irish, explaining the necropolis's title.

Although the day advanced, everything appeared to pause as I inched through the marble town. There was something tranquil about the dead air. No one else lurked around; it seemed like I was the only guy on Earth for a while. It was just the cemetery and me, and for the first time in forever, my mind was free. For the first time in forever, I hadn't thought about her.

My visit of God's acre complete, I made certain to stop by any sections I had missed earlier. I slowly walked atop the asphalt leading to my auto. I felt calm. After a last look around, I climbed in.

About to turn the key, I heard three loud beeps. A text message waited— it could only be one person. I opened the glove compartment, grabbed my cell, and turned it off. A smile took over my mug.

I started the black pickup, backed out of the driveway, and sped off.

6

The Other Tyrel

These walls don't talk—they bitch. All sorts of peeps, screeches, and whines fill my shadowy bedroom. The home's bones must ache as the frosty gusts rattle its windows. But the creaks aren't creepy. Like a grumpy old man, there's a familiarity, an amusing predictability to its complaining. I know what to expect. I've spent the past four moons getting used to this place moan and groan through the early morning hours. Although I may lie awake, I lay this house no blame. After having endured a century of Minnesotan winters, my patience might wear thin, too.

Still, these nocturnal noises are not why I stare at the ceiling until dawn. A trio of recent life changes—fresh digs, new job, newly single—have kept my mind sprinting toward an invisible finish line on most nights. And I can't slow it down.

To a certain degree, I am not alone. My father bears the same problem. He has never slept adequately. Presumably, he is awake right now, smoking a KOOL, sipping on forty weight, and listening to a forgotten talk show. I envision him pacing back and forth atop the worn linoleum of his small kitchen, loudly disagreeing with the last caller. Perhaps I should grab my phone. Dad's always down for breakfast. Hell, I might be the reason he's up in the first place; he worries about me. He'd probably say I'm crazy and tell me to go to bed. Wish I could, Pop. If only I knew how…

Writing, I guess, is the closest I've gotten to slowing my brain's pace. Not only is it a strong wind blowing in my face, hampering my strides, but it's also how I process this mess in my noggin. So where did I put my pen and paper? Ah yes, I remember.

I throw off my comforter. Turning on my bedside lamp, I reach to the floor and snatch the ball point and tablet I had tossed there earlier. I sit up to notice my mother. There she is, on the opposite side of the room, with a giant grin on her grill. And there I am as a baby, wrapped in her arms, being held over a 1980 calendar.

Mom and me

It makes complete sense that I see my mom when I'm about to write. My name actually comes from a Louis L'Amour novel she was reading when I was inside her pregnant belly. And Tyrel Sackett was one of the major players. Only fitting that the boy named after a book character has grown up to be a writer.

Recently, I researched my namesake. Another sleepless night of introspection forced me out of bed and onto Wikipedia. My jaw dropped when I read Tyrel's description. It turns out there were some striking similarities.

To begin, Mr. Sackett was deemed a "black sheep." I chuckled upon viewing this because I recalled when I initially heard it. I once got busted for underage drinking at a party, and my dad had to pick me up. When I arrived home, the only thing my uncle (who was living with us at the time) stated was, "Well, if it isn't the black sheep." My younger brother, of course, had been in all night.

This term came up again several years later. I was visiting a former professor of mine, explaining my frustration with those who follow. I told him most individuals were sheep—they simply do what others do.

"You should be the *black* sheep, break away from the herd, and make your own path," he replied.

His quote still resonates in my ears, and I try my best to heed his suggestion. This could explain why I've lived several times abroad, seeking to carve out tiny niches for myself in the world.

Book Tyrel was further characterized as "compassionate to a fault." This is true in my case. I give people too many chances, the benefit of the doubt when they probably don't deserve it. And I have been burned for being this sparing.

A couple of months ago, I was stood up by a woman. I waited half the damn day for her to show, created generous scenarios in my mind that justified her rudeness (maybe the traffic is bad, or perhaps she got the hour confused), and even called her, only to get her voicemail. Pissed off, I hardly trusted her yarn when I finally spoke with her. My ass she "just forgot." That being said, a few minutes went by on the call, and my anger disappeared. I agreed to meet her the next week, and she left me hanging once again. Part of me is still looking out that window, grinding my teeth.

Eager to learn more, I continued to research Tyrel Sackett. I did a double-take when I reached the end of the paragraph. His last attribute rather embarrassed me.

Naïve where women are concerned, he often seems like a shy schoolboy when facing a pretty girl.

I immediately thought of the lady I've taken on some dates lately. Although I shoot for coolness, I look down whenever she smiles at me. I wriggle around when she asks me personal questions. I really don't prefer to talk about myself, and she knows it. In fact, she calls me out when I get bashful.

"You're getting squirmy," she acknowledges, which perpetuates the awkwardness.

During the occasions when I'm not a nervous Nelson, I love to chat with her about writing. I appreciate her insight on books, not to mention the drafting process itself. She often inquires about the stuff I jot down, and I can usually provide her with answers. But one of her latest questions had me tongue-tied.

"Why haven't you written about yourself?"

She stumped me. Her wringer was admittedly the cause for my restlessness on this night. I couldn't figure it out. I always believed I had described myself. Yet this analytical gal pointed out that my accounts normally focus on other persons, places, or things. I'm in the chronicles, but rarely am I the principal character. In addition, the parts I ultimately reveal about myself are little bits and pieces—like when *she's* attempting to pry.

"What was the inspiration?" she will surely ask when I allude to this narrative.

While I wonder how to reply, I close my notebook, cap my pen, and set them on the floor. I lift my head to spot the third Tyrel in this story. There he is, posing with Mom. My smile mirrors hers.

7

Froze Garden

He wore death like an overcoat. His steps looked excruciating. His wrinkly, emaciated body lurched down the track in zombie fashion. But he kept on creeping on. I put myself in his socks and sandals and sensed my joints flare up after watching his slothful strides. Still, I didn't pity him.

"I've been walking around here for years," the elderly fellow admitted. "And you're the first person I've passed since I don't know when."

I chuckled, but nobody heard—there was not a soul in sight. My lonely laughs drifted across the drifts and vanished into the December air. Back from dreamland, it wasn't a brilliant day at Harriet anymore. Sure, I stopped at the lake's northeast corner again—at the Rose Garden—but the setting seemed entirely different now. The breeze was freezing instead of refreshing, everything green had turned brown, and the old man had been replaced with Old Man Winter. I glanced down at the snow swallowing my boots. I missed my sneakers.

The wind picked up. I shivered. I envisioned Mom quiver. The biting cold of these winters eats her right up. Although she's lived in Minnesota since the mid-1970s, her frail Filipina body still yearns for the tropical climate of her homeland.

"I've never been able to stay warm here," she recently told me.

It came as no surprise that the house often steamed like a sauna when I was a kid.

"Damn it, Beth!" my father would yell. "This isn't the Philippines!"

Despite Pop's complaining, Jack Frost made her jack the thermostat up. And I suddenly dwelled upon how my ex-girlfriend gave me hell for the same reason.

Lyndale Park, Minneapolis, Minnesota

I thought of Amanda. I reflected on our loads of trips together, not to mention the many occasions we visited the Rose Garden. While cracking a smile, I mused on how she used to get frustrated with me for being slow, for snapping countless pictures of the blossoms. I remembered her way ahead on the path, hands on hips, shaking her dome at me. When she ran out of patience, she stomped toward the water and sat on the edge of a nearby dock. No doubt she wanted to dip my digicam into the shallows as opposed to her toes.

Oh yeah, my camera. I removed it from the case slung over my shoulder. I then wondered about Sheik, my best friend in Ecuador. We would bring our cams wherever we explored. She taught me all she knew about photography, continuously pointing out shots I failed to catch.

"That's what it *should* look like," she'd say while comparing her digital screen to mine.

Sheik also advised me in general, and I would glean whatever I could from her. I still did in fact; though over a year had passed since I saw her last.

"I know you are depressed, but you must try to do the things that make you happy, like writing," she urged during a phone conversation not so long ago. "You haven't written in months!"

I relived some of our other chats, including the one we had earlier today, and my subsequent sadness when my minutes expired. She was in the middle of telling me her intentions for Christmas. She planned on traveling to Costa Rica to visit her family and … stupid phone card.

I took a deep breath. I saw it as I exhaled. Kicking up snow, I pictured my boots doing this on the previous night. My brother Jay and I marched from opposite directions, trekking through sleet for several blocks to meet each other for some drinks. We stayed out late, hitting a pair of bars as we caught up. It was fun. I was glad he called. That was nothing new, though. We had been hanging out more than usual—most likely because J checked on me.

"Do you need anything?" he would ask on the phone.

So I wasn't shocked when my cell rang. I was surprised, however, with how far I had come. Had it been September or October, I surely would have refused my brother's offer so I could hole up and mope.

I flashed back to eight weeks before. I recalled myself wandering aimlessly about the Rose Garden, spending countless hours in this serene park in the fall, and strolling along the rows of roses as I roamed the halls of my head. To be honest, I only recognized what had dejected me. The plants may have been flourishing, yet I wasn't. I struggled mightily to accept the reality that I was no longer in the relationship which lasted most of my twenties. There were thousands of fragrant flowers to smell, but I couldn't tell. I was unhappy with what I was doing with my life. Like my endless laps throughout the greenspace, my mind spun in circles. I was a stone's throw from my home, but utterly lost.

Notwithstanding my despondency, the clock stood by me, and so did those who loved me. And I turned the corner. Eventually, the pain lessened, I eased up on myself, and I noticed the little things again, such as the beauty of this charming enclosure. Despite its tiny size, the 1.5-acre lot proved to be a haven; a place that simply offered me space to think, and time to heal.

Consequently, I was here on this wintery day, lumbering through the

Lake Harriet Rose Garden

snow. The Rose Garden stayed loyal to me, so I remained faithful as well. I had continued to stop by whenever I was preoccupied, wanting some exercise, or, in this case, following my dad's advice.

"It's not too bad out," he suggested on the line. "You should go for a walk—probably do you some good."

I further recollected how he broke off the call. During our conversation, my pop repeatedly informed me of his gray cat acting strange, lingering suspiciously around the litter box. Dad kept ignoring the feline until she finally got his complete attention.

"Uh, I gotta go," he confessed right before disconnecting. "I really don't like the look Squeak's giving me."

I chuckled, and nobody heard. But I did not care. It had taken me a while to learn how to laugh again. I would not hold back. Although I was by myself, I didn't feel so lonely anymore.

Lake Harriet Rose Garden

8

A New Dawn

I was done—no dating for me. My last outing ended horrendously. Not only did she insult me multiple times, but the gal proved arrogant enough to assume that I wanted more than the casual basis on which we'd been seeing each other. I would have left her at the bar had I not given her a ride. Someone else could have listened to her ramble on about how "attractive" she thought she appeared; the further she gloated, the more off-putting she became.

"I'll see you in a few weeks," she said before she stepped out of my truck.

"Don't think so," I muttered to myself as I drove off.

The night was awful, but it wasn't all for naught. One positive came from that otherwise wasted Wednesday: I realized that I would never hang out with her again. The closure was nice, especially since I'd had my doubts before. I had important things to focus on anyhow, like my impending trip to Guatemala. I couldn't leave Minnesota soon enough.

Unfortunately, I was still in Minneapolis on Thursday, which wasn't much better than Wednesday. The workday ran late, and I hastily packed while failing to forget the forgettable night before. Tossing and turning well past midnight, I lay disgusted, pissed at myself for not identifying her true colors earlier. But I wouldn't be hurt anymore. My plan was to fly solo for the foreseeable future.

With barely any shuteye, Friday morning slapped me in the mug. My alarm showed 3:30 AM, and I had knives in my eyes. Then I saw them. I could not look away from the striking blue peepers approaching me as I waited in that never-ending line in the Minneapolis-St. Paul International Airport. Her name was Alyssa, and she was volunteering on my Habitat for Humanity trip. That was all the info I had. Unlike the others, I hadn't gotten the opportunity to meet her because she prematurely left our team dinner last month. And I couldn't care less; simply another pretty face.

However, my attitude changed a bit. I figured I should speak to her since she stood next to me, and we had just discovered that our flight to Atlanta had been delayed. We engaged in small talk.

"You don't have to wait for me," she stated at the cafe beyond the metal detectors.

Great; I was clearly on a roll with the ladies. Perhaps I shouldn't have spoken to her. Yet I shook it off.

"I don't mind," I responded. "There's no rush to sit at the gate for a couple of hours."

I hung with her for her coffee cake and mocha, and we ambled to F5.

"So what's your favorite Disney movie?" Alyssa pried right after we sat down.

I paused. Not because I didn't know, but because that was the last question I expected.

"I don't think I've ever been asked that," I replied while chuckling.

After some reminders of titles (I hadn't seen a Disney flick in years), I disclosed that mine was *Mulan,* and she told me hers was *Robin Hood* … before she hummed its theme song. I laughed as she bobbed her head along to her own soundtrack. She was quirky, and I kind of liked it.

To kill the time, we learned about one another. Apart from the basics (stomping grounds, family, job, etc.), we uncovered similar interests. Not only did we both appreciate rock music, but we also enjoyed dancing, and we loved to read. The conversation actually flowed until we suddenly had to discuss more pressing matters.

"Where are you going from Atlanta?" Shelly, my co-leader, inquired as she approached us.

"Wherever you are," I answered. "We're on the same ticket, right?"

Wrong. It turned out she secured a connection to Miami for herself and the team members standing with her as she argued with the airline representative at the counter. Alyssa and I had already gone through security, so we weren't present as our teammates had their itineraries changed. And the employee would not let Shelly speak on our behalf.

For this reason, Alyssa and I attempted to persuade the agent to revise our tickets to match Shelly's. No dice. Our strategy, therefore, would be to find out what we could accomplish in Atlanta. So we boarded the jet with our fellow group members, supposing that everything would get resolved at Hartsfield-Jackson International.

The craft landed a little after 11 AM, and Alyssa and I hit the ground running—literally. Thinking our original connection from Atlanta to Guatemala City might have likewise been postponed, my accomplice convinced me to join her in a mad dash.

"We should run. I've never run through an airport before," she suggested with gigantic eyes. "It will be fun!"

My partner in crime immediately took the lead. Her long, brown hair whipped around as she quickly stomped her knee-high boots across the never-ending terminal. She boldly weaved through the crowds, or simply yelled "excuse me" while plowing down the left side of the escalators. I tried my best to keep up as my carry-on dug into my right shoulder, swinging in all directions from my body.

Despite our valiant effort, Alyssa and I ultimately arrived at the jet bridge to verify that our plane had been off the tarmac for a while. Although we were winded, we were not defeated. We had a backup plan. We would stay overnight in Atlanta, rest up, and catch the 9:50 AM to Guatemala City. There *had* to be two open seats on the morning departure.

"I'm sorry, that flight is full," the woman at the customer service desk revealed.

With nothing else available, Alyssa and I accepted the upcoming 5:30 PM from Atlanta to Los Angeles. From LAX, we would have to board an 11:45 PM to Guatemala City, scheduled to land at 6:30 the following morn. Even though there remained plenty more in store for us, we found solace because our final seats would at least be in first class.

Alyssa and I soon bid goodbye to our eight peers, who were to arrive in Guatemala that evening after a stopover in Miami. Then the two of us wandered about. We stayed busy by playing slapjack over crab cakes and Kamikaze shooters. We also reentered the security checkpoint because we ascended the wrong escalator.

"You can ditch me whenever you want," my companion would occasionally say, assuming (as she eventually confessed) I grew sick of being around her. "It won't bother me."

I would simply laugh and continue walking with her. Not only was I thankful I had an ally during this frustrating situation, but I also dug Alyssa's easy-going, optimistic air. I did not hear her complain once. Her pleasant demeanor made the circumstances much more bearable.

"We'll have a good story to tell anyway," she pointed out during our many treks across the Atlanta airport.

At 7:30 PM, we touched down in Los Angeles. We were exhausted, but in decent spirits yet. We spent most of our layover sitting at the gate, taking silly pictures together and talking as we awaited the last stretch. My new pal never ceased to amuse me either.

"I just want to take a syringe and jab it into your arm!" she admitted while touching one of my protruding veins. "Those would be good arms to start IVs in."

I chuckled as she subsequently described her career in the medical field. Because we got along so easily, we found ourselves boarding the plane in no time.

Following my bud to business class, I collapsed into my cushy seat and sighed — we were finally on our way to Guatemala. Although it was a relief that we'd be reaching our destination at last, the past day, despite its hindrances, wasn't all that bad. Sure, it was a crazy experience, but fortunately I experienced it with someone who made it memorable. I glanced across the aisle at Alyssa. She slumped in her chair, too.

"Is she your wife?" the lady at my three me abruptly asked. She nodded in Alyssa's direction.

"No, but she's my friend," I explained without hesitation.

"Do you want me to trade with her so you can sit together?"

Clouds over Guatemala. Photo by Alyssa Nier.

"Yes, that's very kind of you. Thanks a lot."

Alyssa was my seatmate a minute later. We shared many more laughs, not to mention her headphones. I remember her singing before I nodded off.

After a few hours, I woke up to spot Alyssa taking pictures of the beautiful aurora outside our window. Watching her play with her camera, her presence comforted me. It just felt good to have her there. Noticing I opened my lids, she looked at me. We both smiled.

"What do you think of this one?" she queried while showing me a gorgeous sunrise on her digital's screen.

"That's a great shot. I like it."

And I knew I liked her.

Maybe I wasn't done after all. It really was a new dawn.

9

A Bowl of Fruit

I t was mid-January, but no snow covered the ground—an odd sight for Minnesotans. The seventeen of us were actually in the verdant highlands of Panajachel, Sololá, Guatemala. Teammates on a Global Village trip, we offered our time and sweat on behalf of Twin Cities Habitat for Humanity (based in Minneapolis). And I grew to admire the volunteers who had been at my side the past seven days. From all ages and walks of life, these compassionate men and women left their loved ones, missed work, used vacation hours, and spent their own money to help a pair of families in need of decent, affordable housing. Not only was I proud to have met such good-hearted individuals, it honored me to stand before them.

The scorching afternoon sun blinded me, but that wasn't the reason I wore shades. I hid behind them. I had been in this situation a couple times before. It was the conclusion of the journey, and I was to speak; always an emotional occasion. I knew what to expect, so I focused on my teammates. Their smiles mirrored mine. However, when I glanced at the *guatemaltecos*, who had been working alongside me, the tears started. I couldn't go on.

"Un momentito, por favor," I requested with my eyes down. *A moment, please.*

It was hard saying goodbye. I tried to compose myself while I stared at my feet. I reflected upon the last handful of days. These people had little—in the material sense—but gave their all. They chiseled holes in cinder blocks, mixed cement, and carried heavy buckets of sand at our sides. But they also sang, danced, and laughed with us. They put forth their best effort and, more important, their friendship. By week's end, our newly formed Minnesotan family believed it had become part of a Guatemalan one, too.

Eventually, I gathered myself. I slowly lifted my head. I faced Diego, Estela, Eva Tomasa, Isaías and Jaime (the masons), Manuel, María, Patricia, and Rudy, and thanked them for their kindness. I expressed my hopes to return someday to visit them in their new house. They circled me when I finished. We exchanged handshakes, hugs, and kisses on the cheek.

On my way back to the van, I caught someone moving out of the corner of my eye. Rudy was waving me over to the decrepit, smoky shack his family had been living in for so many years. He said his mother wanted to see me. I followed his open hand and squinted into the casa. I barely saw María's silhouette in front of a wooden table. She appeared to be preparing something. Suddenly, she spun around and began walking toward me, her stout figure more visible with every step. When she finally emerged from the darkness, she sported the ear-to-ear grin I had gotten used to. In her hands was a bowl of fruit. She handed it to me.

"Gracias por todo," she stated with a teary smile. *Thanks for everything*.

Too choked up to talk, the only thing I could do was give her a huge embrace before I sadly exited her home.

House dedication. Photo by Alyssa Nier.

Constantly replaying this image in my mind, I wept on the ride back to the hotel. I gazed at the food, truly struck by María's generosity.

It turned out this assortment of bananas, strawberries, and oranges was the reason she disappeared earlier in the day. Putting her hectic household duties aside, she made a special trip to buy this gift for my team—even though she hardly had the cash to spare. A *tazón de fruta* may not seem like much to some, but it meant the world to me.

With a few Habitat International trips under my belt, I've noticed a recurring result. Teams travel with the purpose of building homes, but construction isn't all that happens. Invaluable learning experiences occur, and intercultural friendships take root. Everlasting memories are created as well. And even the smallest gestures, like an offering of fruit, can leave the deepest impressions.

Antigua, Sacatepéquez, Guatemala

10

An Afternoon in Antigua

The temp was mild, but my fever wasn't. I was burning up, in fact. My pulse raced. And my eyes stung from the sweat, which also heavily salted my mouth. Still, the sourness lingering on my buds tasted better than last night's dinner. Whoever had prepared my meal hadn't done so sanitarily. My insides had been turning inside out since the wee hours.

Yet I remained determined—no way I would relax. My camera was ready, and I had learned from previous travels that second looks weren't guaranteed. Too many things could happen from then on. Plans might change, I may become distracted, forget my cam, or the weather could be inclement. Right then was an opportune moment for pictures. So I forewent a much-needed nap to capture the beauty of Antigua, Guatemala.

It was midafternoon, and I stood in the middle of the city. The majestic Volcán de Agua towered from the south. It seemed like the colossal volcano watched me as I circled the square. I sauntered the tree-lined paths of Central Park, taking in the sounds of a five-piece band, giggling children, and water peacefully flowing from the reconstructed fountain at the plaza's bull's-eye. Weak from food poisoning, I meandered until my legs became too wobbly. I had to rest. I perched on the fount's edge for a while and observed my surroundings.

To the north sat El Palacio del Noble Ayuntamiento; both stories fronted by many stout arches. The national flag and Sacatepéquez Department banner proudly stood atop city hall. I glanced right. La Catedral de Santiago gleamed on Parque Central's eastern boundary. It was immaculate. The manner in which the ivory church brilliantly shined in the afternoon sun captivated me. I looked behind me. El Palacio de los Capitanes Generales presided over Plaza Mayor's southern border. Already having read it was the center of the Spanish colonial government in Central America, its almighty presence did not surprise me. The double-arcaded, two-story office building powerfully loomed above the cobblestones. I faced west to study the colorful, antiquated structures lining Fifth Avenue. Intrigued, I took a deep breath, rose to my feet, and decided to see where the road would lead me.

It didn't take me long to know something felt wrong. I became light-headed as I headed north, my steps grew heavier as I crossed Fourth, and I was beat by the time I passed Third Street. I was in awful shape. My joints started to ache. Beads of perspiration trickled down my face. About to drop, I stumbled upon an entertaining stopping point.

Halfway down the block, dozens of people surrounded a performer. The crowd roared as a mime juggled atop his unicycle. The Guatemalan put on quite the display. He jumped, twirled, and zigzagged while somehow maintaining his balance. Impressed with his act, I ignored my symptoms for a moment. I stepped in front of my fellow onlookers to frame his *fotografía*. He saw me immediately. But instead of looking away, the young man posed as he pedaled toward me, putting his right mitt on his hip and his left behind his head. I fought off laughter, steadied my camera, and snapped the mime's photo just before he spun around.

The show was impressive, but I had to go on. Rather queasy now, I staggered across Second, snaking through blurry pedestrians till I couldn't anymore. I halted. I was huffing and puffing. Nevertheless, my body wasn't the only thing that stopped me near the avenue's northern end. I had more sightseeing to do. Gasping to catch my wind, I checked out the Santa Catalina arch, which spanned the width of Fifth. My hotel bed called me while I examined the colonial curve. I was run-down, but too drained to run. So I sluggishly ambled on.

I reached a T and turned left. Despite my ever-worsening illness, I continued to delay my return to the inn. I just tottered a block before pausing anew. On the corner of First Street West and Sixth Avenue North boomed the magnificent Iglesia La Merced. In awe, I ogled the ornate yellow facade of this church for several minutes before finally clicking a picture. It would be my last of the day.

Shortly thereafter, I shoved open the door to my room at Posada Los Búcaros. I frantically removed the camera case strapped over my shoulder, kicked off my shoes, and dived underneath my bedding. Although it was

Iglesia La Merced in the distance

summerlike outside, I lay freezing. I threw on another shirt. I shivered until I passed out.

Within a few days, I was back in the States, recovered and reliving my trip to Guatemala as I eagerly perused my pics. When I came across the images from Antigua, however, they instantly reminded me of my ailing afternoon. I almost sensed my stomach churn and my forehead get hot. Because my condition worsened before it improved, I failed to embark on anymore photo excursions before leaving the country.

But the shots also stirred up the positives. Revisiting Antigua in my mind, I roamed its cobblestone streets, admired the colonial structures, and appreciated its striking colors. I proceeded to Parque Central, weaved through the arches of the surrounding buildings, and grabbed a seat at the relaxing fountain. I soaked in the tranquil ambience, gazed at the tremendous Volcán de Agua and realized how lucky I was. Where else can a person stroll through a park eclipsed by a 3800-meter-tall volcano?

So I reflected upon my choice from that Saturday — trading soundness for snapshots — and wondered if I had made the correct move. On one hand, I disregarded my health, and paid for it. I shivered when I thought of the chills I had that evening. On the other hand, I spent an afternoon touring incredible Antigua; an opportunity I may never get again.

I scrolled through my photos once more. I sighed.

The price was well worth it.

11

Spared

The February sun was about to rise when we bid our goodbyes. The AM was cold and quiet. Aside from the few words spoken between us, not a sound could be heard in the neighborhood; Uptown wasn't up yet. We hugged. I wished Alyssa well, and we kissed. My girlfriend stepped into her Hyundai, backed up, and zoomed off. I watched her taillights disappear into the wintry dawn.

In the snowy alley behind my home, I thought about what she said before closing her door: "good luck." I would need it. In fact, I had to change a tire on an icy road before I could even leave for work. Be that as it may, I was already lucky perhaps; a topic we discussed during last night's conversation.

"Someone's watching over you," Alyssa told me.

And as I recalled yesterday's narrow escape, I couldn't have agreed more.

I was on the inside track, heading home from my job, when I figured I was a goner. The tail of my pickup suddenly swung into the middle lane of Interstate 94 West. Fortunately, no one was next to me. But I wasn't in the clear. Furiously zigzagging, I knew I was screwed. So I focused on damage control—opting to take myself out rather than others—and yanked hard to the left. Boom! At 60 MPH, I slammed into the massive snow bank preceding the concrete barrier. A cloud of slush exploded in the air and covered the hood of my Ford Ranger. The seatbelt dug into my clavicle, keeping me just inches away from greeting the helm with my face. My heart raced. I desperately tried to

Sundial by Lake Harriet

catch my breath as I swiveled my skull around, peering through the cab's windows to determine if the crash had affected anyone else. At best, I expected a gawker slowdown or state troopers who had been called by witnesses, or at least a Good Samaritan. There was no change in traffic, though. Apparently, my big scare was not that rare. I tugged my restraint off. I got out.

Because of the slickness of the shoulder, I clung to the truck, grabbing it with one hand while cautiously circling the vehicle. Much to my surprise, I noticed no dings, scratches, or missing pieces. The snow pile cushioned me somehow. Not only did I survive the accident unscathed, but my pickup apparently did, too. I let out a tremendous sigh of relief. I climbed into the Ford, reversed out of the bank, flicked my right blinker on, and smoothly rejoined traffic like nothing had occurred.

But something had transpired. Later that evening, I stepped out of the house, on my way to visit Alyssa. As I approached my auto, I saw it leaning toward the middle of Garfield Avenue. I detected a slight hissing sound near the engine. I took a few steps closer and discovered a deflated driver's side tire. Given the Goodyear remained buried in the snow during my once-over on 94's edge, I failed to spot the banana-shaped piece now missing along the rim. I decided to wait till daylight to put the spare on.

The boulevard strips bulged with drifts, which pushed the parked cars closer to the center of the road. So I would almost be in line with someone's undercarriage while I toiled. It was awfully risky to crouch in the middle of the street in the obscurity. I called Alyssa, and she came to my place instead.

When she left the following morn, I made a beeline for my banger. Unbeknownst to me, this project, which I originally estimated would last under a half hour, would reach almost four. First, my jack broke, and my housemate didn't have a hoist, of course. I subsequently phoned my dad. We raised the Ranger with one of his lifts, and it immediately fell off, causing us to jump backward in fright. After placing the lift in a different location, we successfully elevated the vehicle, and changed the flat. But we were far from done. Thanks to the black ice under the Ford, the stickshift spun in place for what seemed like an eternity. (Damn rear-wheel drive.) We rocked the automobile back and forth and chipped away several inches of ice from around all the rollers with the claw of a framing hammer until we freed the truck. Then I drove it to a nearby repair shop. It was approximately 10:30 AM when the mechanic informed me that I'd have a new wheel by afternoon's end.

I practically nodded off in my office an hour later. (My roomie, who rode the bus to work, generously let me borrow her Jeep.) I propped my head up with my palm to scan my attire: dark dress pants, a gray button-down shirt, a black tie, and charcoal loafers. Provided that I began the day under two layers of thermals, jeans, a hooded sweatshirt, a winter coat, a stocking cap, wool socks, and steel-toe boots, I appreciated the lightweight apparel I now donned. The heavy load I had been wearing, coupled with the energy I exerted in those duds, had drained me. I laughed in disbelief about how long it took me to get my ride to the garage.

Yet I wasn't at all upset. I felt quite fortunate. Weighing my close call against what might have happened, I would always opt for the same outcome. No cops, no accident report, no increased insurance, and, thankfully, no other victims. But most important, I was alive and well. I *was* lucky. And I'd undoubtedly welcome all the difficulty I had with the spare because, in all honesty, I believed someone had spared me.

12

On Call

I woke up to a series of loud beeps and a yawn. The mattress was suddenly a tad higher on my left. I reached over. She wasn't there. I slowly opened my eyes to the moonlight filtered by the window blinds faintly illuminating the room. Just beyond the foot of the bed, I saw her curvy silhouette fumbling through the dresser drawers. She turned around and approached me. Her lips touched mine. She vanished once again.

Six — the number of instances she had left me … over a weekend. There was no stopping her. Without hesitation, my girlfriend would spring from the covers, jump into her clothes, and dash out the door. And I uttered no words because I knew she had no choice. It was part of her gig, after all.

As a cardiovascular technologist, Alyssa "assists physicians in coronary angioplasties and [helps apply] stents in people with heart disease." Normally working four tens, she hustles through the halls of Abbott Northwestern on Mondays, Tuesdays, Wednesdays, and Fridays, from 7 AM to 5:30 PM. But sometimes she is "on call", which means she might have to return to the institution at any point from the moment her normal shift ends (usually at 5:30) until 7 AM the subsequent morning. When on call, she must carry a pager and immediately drop everything in the event she's summoned when somebody is "in the middle of a heart attack." Patients can arrive from many places throughout Minnesota and Wisconsin since Abbott has connections with other medical centers. And given that being on standby is a unique situation, some distinctive pros and cons come with the territory.

According to Alyssa, one positive is "being able to see the difference [she's] making in sick patients' lives" in the flesh. She enjoys the challenge, claiming to sense a sudden burst of energy because the subjects are really ill, and the team — a Registered Nurse (RN), Cardiovascular Technologist (CVT), Radiologic Technologist (RT), and an Interventional Cardiologist — are trying to save them. She also likes the money, earning 1.5 times her regular hourly wage for every occasion she gets beeped. Therefore, if wanting to make a lot of dough in a short period, she can pick up a call weekend; 5:30 PM Friday to 7 AM Monday.

With this in mind, there are significant downsides to being on alert. First, even though she experiences a rush when attempting to rescue ailing patients, the cases do not always end smoothly. She has seen many die over the past three years.

"You feel bad for the families, but [death] is part of the job," she states. "You take your moment — whether it's going to the bathroom or eating lunch by yourself — and deal with it."

Another huge negative is that she can't arrange concrete plans … ever. Provided that she has only thirty minutes to show up after being requested, Alyssa has to stay close to home so she can report by phone ("This is Alyssa Nier calling to check in," she confirms to the receptionist), throw on her work duds (T-shirt, tennis shoes, and scrub pants), and hit the road in her Hyundai Sonata. (She often drives 80-85 MPH to Abbott, which is only eight miles from her apartment.) She hates "getting called in during the middle of the night when [she's slated for] a ten-hour shift the next day" and becomes frustrated because those outside her field cannot identify with her duties.

Her position is physically demanding because she wears five-pound lead aprons, moves patients onto tables, and stays on her feet for most of her turns. Her occupation is psychologically taxing because lives are constantly at stake. A wrong move, like injecting an air bubble, could kill someone. And plenty of individuals cannot comprehend being at the hospital's disposal.

"I have to be mentally prepared," she insists. "When my pager goes off, I got to go. [People in general] just don't get it."

I, in all honesty, failed to understand initially.

It was hard adjusting to my partner's sporadic schedule at first. Alyssa would be with me one second and gone the following; sometimes during the wee hours. Or I would catch her in passing. (She once held the front gate of her building open just long enough for me to enter before she hurried off to the office.) In order to know why she had to ditch me at points, I asked her to give me the details of her profession. So she explained to me the nitty-gritty. In addition, she feared that I would grow tired of the on-again-off-again.

"I'm afraid one day you'll get sick of waiting around for me and my busy schedule ... and you'll leave," she confessed.

However, I'll still be in bed, no matter what time she comes home.

I recognize my inability to grasp Alyssa's daily grind unless I actually do it. But because I love her, I will try my best to learn more regarding her very specialized vocation. This piece was one way of doing so. And hopefully, this story sheds light on her career as well.

13

Nokomis

It was midafternoon on a Thursday. The gas smacked the floor. Just leaving the Mall of America, I couldn't get home soon enough. I needed some space. The mad hordes of MOA never failed to annoy me. While I hustled north on Highway 77, I abruptly made a pit stop. I drove close to a familiar face—an old chum I hadn't seen in several moons. So I forewent the exit to 62 West and stayed the course on Cedar Avenue. Near my destination, I suddenly relived a conversation from months earlier.

Autumn had recently arrived, and it was my friend's birthday. I, along with a handful of her closest pals, joined Lena to celebrate her 29th at a local watering hole. I shook my head in disbelief when I realized how everything had blazed by. It seemed like yesterday when I bought Lena drinks for her 22nd after studying for a summer in Venezuela with her. And similar to that night in 2002, her boyfriend, Dave, now sat next to me. Those two had remained good friends of mine ever since our early days. The reality that some things never changed comforted me. This comfort, however, eventually disappeared.

I grew goose bumps. Feeling the chill of the evening, I wished I had worn an extra layer. I expressed my displeasure with summer's end to Dave. But he reserved his opinion until Jack Frost entered the discussion.

"Do you like winter?" he asked me.

A miracle prevented me from spitting out my ale.

"Not a chance," I answered after forcing my beer down. "I've been living in the wrong state my entire life. It's one of the reasons why I go to Latin

America every year."

"Huh. Well, I love it!"

"Not me. I'd take hot over cold any day."

"No way, gimme the cold! I'm that guy you see walking around Lake Nokomis in the dead of winter."

"You're nuts!"

I hated wintertime in Minnesota, however, I only bashed the season Dave referred to—I wasn't knocking the place. In fact, I ogled Nokomis at the very moment I got out of my truck.

Minneapolis proved unusually mild on this St. Patrick's Day. Although the temperature hike was rare, I believed it to be fair. Perhaps this was Mother Nature's idea of making up for last winter's quick start. (I remembered my disgust when flakes touched the ground in October.) I itched to be outdoors. Weak throughout the past week, I holed up on account of pounding headaches, incessant sneezing, and a nose that wouldn't stop running. I was going to capitalize on the warm weather because I was finally getting over my cold.

It was a bit breezy, and an air of familiarity swirled around me the second my feet hit the track. I had been coming here so long for a couple of different reasons. First, I loved the scenery. Lined with umbrageous trees and well-maintained lawns, the area was lush in the spring and summertime, and decorated with striking colors in the fall. I also liked the extra legroom—the trails were never swamped. Rarely having to step aside for saunterers, joggers, baby strollers, and dogs, I could amble at my own pace along its three miles of footpath. The same went for this afternoon, too. Hardly anyone else schlepped in sight.

Skirting the thawing shoreline, I reminisced about happy memories there. I recalled the many instances I rushed from work to soak in the park's beauty on a sunny day … and how I often tried to capture its allure. I thought about my habit of carrying a camera on my strolls, which conjured up peaceful afternoons of snapping photos of the beaches, bridges, and boats. While I observed the fields along the western edge, I recollected the seasons of softball I enjoyed on the lakeside diamonds. My smile grew bigger when I flashed on the last occasion I played. It was a Saturday in mid-September, and my team won half a dozen games in a row to claim the league championship.

The greenspace had additionally been a refuge for me through my rough patches. If I was brainstorming job leads during periods of unemployment, coping with depression, or battling writer's block, I had come to the drink to think. I must have legged hundreds of miles racking my brain over the years. Not only did the tranquil ambience help me process my thoughts, but it never ceased to put my mind at ease. I always experienced peace after circling the

Lake Nokomis Park, Minneapolis, Minnesota

banks. And I encountered the same sensation on this visit as well.

Satisfied with yet another lap under my belt, I returned to the Ranger an hour later. I glanced back at the lake. Although no snow surrounded it, most of the water remained frozen. I stared at the ice and replayed my chat with Dave on his lady's birthday. Images of his frigid laps immediately came to mind. There was obviously something special about the locale which lured him there in subzero temps, repeatedly. I fired up the engine, aware for the first time that—apart from his wintertime treks—I could relate to Dave's attraction to the loch. I mulled over this commonality as I exited the lot.

The shores now in my rearview, I reflected on the countless occasions they had drawn me in. There lingered no doubt that the lake had been a constant for me. Through pleasant stretches, sad spells, or whether I was simply appreciating the weather, I continued to return to Nokomis.

Maybe Dave wasn't so crazy after all.

14

Lucky Man

She had never seen this place. And I hadn't either—not during this season, anyway. To me, there was no reason to visit Minnehaha Falls this early on the calendar. The temps always sank low, and there was too much snow. But things were different on this last Sunday in March—a rare warm pocket floated over Minneapolis. Apart from a few scattered dying drifts, there was hardly any white in sight. In fact, most of the remaining pack clung to the rocky embankment along the backside of the cascade. The sun struggled to reach its shadowy walls.

Alyssa and I crossed the bridge above the 53-foot cataract, donning thin jackets. We joined dozens of fellow sightseers on the concrete ledge atop the north side. Everything around appeared brown—not a postcard panorama in the slightest. Notwithstanding the drab landscape, there was something charming about Minnehaha. The melody produced by the light rapids gave the weir an air of tranquility. Lured by its lullaby, we went into the abyss for a closer look.

We descended a nearby stairway to a cement platform overlooking the chute's shallow pool, which appeared knee-deep. However, it wasn't the mere's mere size that interested us. A woman sharing the landing mentioned that the ice behind the waterfall sported a bluish hue. Intrigued, we were about to climb the iron railing when we agreed that it might not be such a good idea. Alyssa's flip-flops weren't ideal for the jagged, slippery, unfenced path to the colorful crystals. We decided to stick to the crick flowing away from the frosty enclosure instead.

Staying the course proved tricky as we followed Minnehaha Creek. The trail was thawing, so it comprised alternating solid and muddy patches, not to mention occasional puddles. Alyssa and I carefully planned our next moves, stepping, lunging, and frequently jumping from dry spot to dry spot. We grabbed the branches of surrounding trees to stay out of the muck most times. Still, the challenging track didn't faze us. Rather than complain about bouncing, we made a game out of our Sunday stroll. We actually enjoyed leaping throughout the afternoon.

When not concentrating to keep her toes from getting wet, Alyssa focused her lens. She regularly took pictures along the brook. While surveying the leafless landscape, she would carefully tilt her camera—holding it at just the right angle for several seconds—before clicking the shutter button. Then she'd immediately show me the scenes displayed on her digital's screen.

"What do you think about this one?" she would wonder.

And I could see her practice paid off. I thought about her earlier pictures I had reviewed, and it was very clear that her photography had improved. The images she just snapped turned out nicely framed and centered; a drastic

Minnehaha Falls

change from the completely random, slapdash pics I had been used to scrolling through.

As we marched toward the Mississippi River (half a mile east of the falls), we came upon a prodigious puddle comparable to the size of the pool at the base of the cascade. The right offered nothing but mud. The left led to the mucky bank of the stream. We took a few steps in both directions, simply to return to the land preceding the spill. Alyssa contemplated her sopping sandals.

"Perhaps another day," she said.

So we doubled back to the cataract. We retraced our skips along the swampy walk, playing as we did previously. We held hands. She burst into song. I ruined her tunes with my awful voice. We poked fun at each other. Besides our normal banter, we took turns holding the camera high above our heads to snap goofy selfies. We returned to the falls in no time because we enjoyed ourselves so much. We admired the shoot again for a bit, and I asked my companion for her opinion of Minnehaha Park.

"I like it," she replied. "There's this beautiful waterfall right in the middle of the cities. That's pretty cool."

I processed what Alyssa pointed out and realized I had taken this

Minnehaha Creek

location for granted. Given I had grown up in the area, I never pondered the uniqueness of this urban cascade. To live within minutes of such an alluring site was "pretty cool" after all. But that wasn't the primary reason I believed to be so fortunate.

I turned to Alyssa. As she watched the water, I reflected on that fateful weekend in January when we unexpectedly crossed paths. After seeing where life had taken us from that point, I was truly grateful that we were together in those airports for twenty-six hours. Even though it only had been two and a half months since we first met, I honestly felt like I had known her for ages. And I couldn't imagine being without her.

I was a lucky man.

15

Rose Garden

Alyssa grabs her forks from the bottom. Because we place the utensils we've washed most recently on top of the others, my girlfriend always reaches far into the drawer, pulling the silverware from the base of the tray "so they all get used" when she eats. I laughed about her quirkiness while staring out my office window. My smirk soon turned upside down, though. The thought of her mannerisms further saddened me.

Alyssa had gone, and all was wrong. I had been without her for five days, and she'd be touring the Alps for five more, which seemed like five lifetimes. Never had I missed someone this much. I could barely function—eating and sleeping proved daunting. I forced myself to go to work each morning, believing my job would somehow take my mind off her. But I was mistaken.

Despite my efforts to occupy myself, I wasted away in a vacant building instead of her apartment. I failed to focus. Hell, I couldn't concentrate even if I wanted to; there just wasn't a ton to do at Humboldt Secondary School. The kids had taken their finals a week earlier, the only staff around was the occasional janitor, and summer classes remained a fortnight ahead. So I used the better part of my lonely days attempting to recruit tutors via email, look at spreadsheets, and wander three stories of desolate hallways. However, the emptiness that filled the corridors was fitting—it matched the void consuming my soul. I was so lost without her.

Desperate for familiarity, I closed my laptop earlier than usual on

Wednesday. I refused to rot in my workplace anymore. After locking Room 2264, I quickly left the building, jumped into my truck, and raced out of the parking lot. I knew exactly where to drive.

Twenty minutes later, I parallel parked on Roseway Road in Minneapolis. I stepped out of the Ranger and realized it had been months since my last visit. In fact, things appeared quite different this time around. It was a picturesque day in mid-June, and the roses were in bloom. All that had died in December now thrived. Vibrant hues decorated the property rather than the wintry whites, grays, and browns. And dozens of individuals perused the premises; not just me on this occasion. I hastened my pace as I approached the liveliness of Lyndale Park.

It was good to be back. Similar to my countless summertime visits of yesteryear, I spent the next hour studying the Rose Garden. I admired the periwinkle, fuchsia, and amber blossoms while I weaved between the yard's sixty-two central flower beds. I paused frequently to not only breathe in the petals' sweet-smelling aromas but also to observe the billowy clouds wafting across the powder blue sky. Then I circled the Heffelfinger Fountain that

Lyndale Park Rose Garden, Minneapolis, Minnesota

proudly stood atop the patio. Listening to the water peacefully flow from the mouths of the Greco-Roman busts, which adorned the marble and bronze bubbler, had a calming effect on me. I took a deep breath and took in my surroundings. At last, I felt more like myself—things weren't so bad after all. I contently headed toward my Ford.

Before I got in my vehicle, I stood with the door open to survey the Rose Garden anew. The grounds sparkled. The late-afternoon sun enhanced the dazzling colors of the bushes. Awestruck by the park's beauty, I was happy with my decision to leave work early. I pondered how this special place always made everything OK as I climbed into my pickup.

About to turn the key, I noticed my phone buzzing against my thigh. I reached into my pocket and read the caller ID. A grin swept across my grill.

The screen showed Austria.

16

My Only Job

T his is my last day!"
I spun away from my laptop to see a frustrated undergrad stomp through the door.

"What happened?" I pried.

"They couldn't stay on task!"

"That's too bad."

"It is. I'm going to borrow a pen."

She darted to my desk and snatched a ballpoint. She hustled to the three-ring binder atop the file cabinet on the other side of my office, furiously flipped through its pages, and hastily recorded her last hours as an English tutor.

"Is this your *only* job?" she inquired before abruptly turning her back to me.

With her question still registering, I reclined in my rolling chair. I bit my tongue while she walked out.

Spending the next several minutes pondering what she said, I reflected upon all the hard work I had put in to start the program she just quit. I was a little upset. But I soon shrugged it off—it wasn't about me. I refocused on the almost 20,000 students in Minnesota's capital city who were not proficient in mathematics or reading. They deserved my attention. They were the reason for my occupation.

The Saint Paul Public Schools Foundation created my Tutoring Coordinator position with the goal of increasing proficiency in math, science, and literacy at Humboldt Secondary; a diverse, 7-12 institution in the West Side neighborhood. Because of lack of space, the principal asked me to use the "push in" model. The tutors—required to contribute at least an hour per week—were to act as "floats", i.e., assist the teacher by moving around the classroom to help pupils.

However, starting my VISTA (Volunteers in Service to America) year at the end of November wasn't ideal. The Thanksgiving and Christmas breaks were huge recruiting roadblocks; people focused on the holidays, not tutoring. And no one seemed willing to brave the biting winter to offer their time at Humboldt. So 2010 got off to a slothful start.

Zero volunteers had shown up through January. In February, I did a handful of orientations, but still no tutelage had occurred. Yet I remained persistent, and my steadfast recruiting—countless emails, phone calls, and meetings—eventually paid off.

At the conclusion of March, I had four. I added thirteen to the roster in April. By June 30, twenty-three individuals had consistently tutored in Humboldt math, science, and literacy classes. Despite those first dismal months, I had gotten a system up and running after all. Other people noticed as well.

On the last afternoon of summer school, one of the English teachers approached me.

"I can't tell you how much your tutor has helped me," he admitted. "Thank you."

Then he shook my hand.

I smiled. Although it was a slight gesture, the handshake reminded me of why I wanted to be a VISTA in the first place: to make a difference.

Is this my only job?

Yes, and I'm proud of it.

17

Playing Hooky

Summer classes were over, but summer definitely wasn't. It was the last Monday in July, the ten o'clock hour hadn't arrived, and my T-shirt was already clinging to me. The school was sweltering. Because there was no air conditioning, the building had been a furnace since May's end. But my two months of enduring Humboldt's heat didn't matter. Even though I had been accustomed to dripping on the job, I was hotter than usual on this morn.

When I showed up at work, the secretary informed me of my room assignment for the fall. I spent the initial hours of the day exerting myself—lugging my belongings from my former office on the second floor to my new one on the first. And 1253 provided no view. The lack of a draft (at least I got an occasional breeze in old 2264), along with the heavy lifting I had done that dawn, drastically enhanced my perspiration. I was sopping and seeking fresh air. So I went outside.

I traipsed to my truck, rolled down the windows, and hopped in. Yet this wouldn't do. I just couldn't stare at that stifling school. In need of a change of scenery—something besides that brown-bricked dungeon of empty classes, barren walls, and humid halls—I decided to play hooky.

I started the engine, barreled east down Morton, and hung a right on Robert. Various destinations ran through my brain while Humboldt disappeared from my rearview. When I ditched St. Paul for West St. Paul, one image kept budging to the forefront of my mind: the wooden sign marking the entrance to Thompson County Park. It was a place I had passed countless times

Thompson Lake, West St. Paul, Minnesota

before but had never visited. Now was the perfect opportunity to check it off my list. I turned left onto Butler.

A few ticks later, I pulled up to Thompson Lake—a small, quiet pond circled by overhanging branches and cattails. I stepped out of the Ranger and ambled to the charming rain garden between the pedestrian track and parking lot. Impressed by the pretty plot of wildflowers, ferns and sedges, I walked to the fishing dock. I peered off the pier to watch a handful of ducks glide atop the calm water for several minutes. Relaxed by the tranquil ambience, I retreated to shore. I embarked on the footpath, excited for what else the park had in store.

Notwithstanding the blinding sun overhead, the varied vegetation intrigued me. The plants ascended away from the passage. I smelled the sharp scent of recently cut lawn and noticed that a few feet of short grass bordered the trail on both sides. It appeared that somebody made one run with a mower along each edge of the walkway. The next step of foliage comprised thick, green bushes that occasionally sported colorful flowers. The patches of yellow, orange, and purple blossoms that sporadically poked through the dense shrubbery fascinated me. Tall trees loomed over the hedges, too. They formed a forested wall that closed me off from the rest of the world. There were trunks, limbs, and leaves as far as I could see. I eagerly pressed on.

I slowly hiked across the verdant labyrinth while the morning rays intensified. Constantly wiping the sweat off my brow with my forearm, I stopped frequently to not only catch my breath but also to decide which path to follow at the many bifurcations I encountered. The course I chose eventually took me out of Thompson and to another greenspace.

I crossed the arch over Highway 52 and descended into Kaposia Park. Suddenly standing within the limits of South St. Paul, I scanned the area. There was a softball field, Frisbee golf, endless trees, and additional routes. Despite the powerful urge to attack the pathways ahead, guilt stopped me in my tracks. I was supposed to be working, even if that simply meant monitoring my emails for the ensuing month. Remorseful for being AWOL, I opted to double back.

I discovered a map I previously overlooked when I returned to the lake an hour after leaving it. Recalling the endless arteries I had bypassed, I studied the grid to find out which lines I had skipped. I soon learned I had merely traversed the tip of the iceberg.

Much to my surprise, I realized that Thompson was a 57-acre woodland. Although I earned a living in nearby St. Paul, and grew up in adjacent Inver Grove Heights, I never knew West St. Paul hid such a large recreation ground. I shook my head in disbelief as I climbed into my pickup.

While I drove back to Humboldt, I practically sweated just thinking of my oven for an office. Plus, the dog days of August were yet to come. But the sultriness wouldn't dampen my mood.

I could always take another break. And there remained many more paths to explore.

Thompson County Park, West St. Paul, Minnesota

18

Four Months

We were just strides into our jog when Alyssa collapsed. She wailed. Noticing a wasp loudly buzzing overhead, I hunched while I rushed to her. Tears gushed down her face.

"I got stung!" she cried.

I removed her hand from her neck. At the base of her skull appeared a swollen, quarter-sized welt.

"Are you allergic?"

"No, but it really hurts!"

"C'mon, let's get you back to the car."

I reached down to pick her up and THWACK! I dropped as well. The same headhunting wasp nailed me below the crown of my noggin. Fortunately, I didn't require an EpiPen either.

I returned to Normandale Lake ninety days later, strolling over that dark stretch of path once again. I wasn't concerned, though, for it was cool outside. However, allowing that the early November temps had killed off the wasps, something far worse than a vespine had leveled my family. And my father endured the brunt of it.

A few weeks earlier, my brother and I found our dad jaundiced and unable to rise out of bed. Jay and I were absolutely beside ourselves. We basically carried our pop into the vehicle and drove him to the VA against his will. The practitioners soon discovered a mass on his pancreas. Although they inserted a stent to keep the tumor from pushing against the blood vessel supplying his liver, my father (whose yellow complexion eventually disappeared thanks to the procedure) had to withstand several more tests over his three-day hospital stay so the doctors could determine the seriousness of his condition. Their conclusion proved crushing.

Waterfall at Normandale Lake

Dad was going to die. He received a diagnosis of Stage IV pancreatic cancer, given, "based on averages", a prognosis of four months. FOUR MONTHS. My world crumbled the second the horrible news came from the oncologist's mouth. Not only was I terrified of losing my best friend, but I also profoundly worried for him. I couldn't fathom what had to be running through his mind. I was afraid he was afraid.

But Pop accepted it. Based on his stoic demeanor upon exiting the hospital, I figured he must have known it was coming. He confessed from his passenger seat that he wasn't scared at all. He simply desired two things: no pain and to be at home.

After helping him set up hospice care, I remained at my old man's side ever since that dreadful morn; until this day that is, when he insisted I have some space to myself. He recommended I go to Normandale because Alyssa and I had recently moved into a place near the tranquil waters in Bloomington. He had fond memories of when he would take Jay and me there when we were little.

My dad's suggestion was on the ball like usual. Despite the dense fog I had been in lately, my vision cleared, albeit temporarily, because of the picturesque scenery of Mt. Normandale Lake Park. The morning sun glared. The fall colors struck me, and the slight breeze refreshed me. I started by the now wasp-free crime scene, proceeded on the tree-covered trail, and inhaled deep breaths of the crisp, clean autumn air. I often stopped to peer over countless cattails, transfixed by the glistening surface of the small (under two miles of shoreline) loch. As I walked off the past weeks, I subdued my anxiety with images of the good old days, back to lakeside jaunts with my pop. I immediately thought of our favorite spot, quickening my steps.

I soon arrived at Normandale's centerpiece—the tiny waterfall on the southeastern curve. Relaxed by the murmur of the cascade, I closed my eyes. I pictured Jay and me alongside our father two decades before. My brother normally climbed on the rocky banks while I fished with Dad downstream from the falls. I laughed when I recalled how he always used to bait my hooks. A ring abruptly opened my lids. I dug my cell from my jacket pocket. It was Alyssa, phoning me from work.

"Whatcha doin'?"

"Walking around Normandale."

"Really? Why?"

"Pop made me."

"Good! You need to take care of yourself, too."

"Yeah, yeah, that's what he said."

"I know; I just talked to him."

"Figures. I still can't believe this is happening."

"Me neither, but you have to focus on the time you have left with him."

She was right. When the call ended, I finished the rest of my lap with a new sense of purpose. I would make the most of those four months.

Pop and Alyssa

19

Pals

I was painting the spare bedroom. My dad, who enjoyed watching me fix up his rickety double-wide, could still BS with me from his hospital bed in the adjoining living room. Despite being in different parts of the trailer, we maintained a constant flow of convo through the doorway between us.

"What do you think, Pop?"

"Looks good."

"Yeah, it's coming along. I'll need to put on a second…"

Hearing the doorknob turn, a familiar greeting suddenly interrupted me.

"Heeellooo!"

My father beamed instantly.

"Hey, Alyssa!"

"Nice sweatshirt! Where did you get it?"

"Some gal gave it to me," he answered with a wink.

He reached his arms out, and my girlfriend promptly hugged him as usual. She visited me for a kiss and went back to Dad. She grabbed her normal seat on the tattered armchair beside him.

I remembered my roller and focused on resurrecting the decades-old paneling. I made certain to tune in.

Although I stayed busy slapping white on my pop's off-white walls, I tried my best to listen in on their discussion. In all honesty, I couldn't help but eavesdrop; their chats always entertained me. On this January afternoon, they jointly joked about the shameless guests on the series of judge shows my father viewed each weekday. It was their thing.

"Who takes someone to court over a [video game console]?!" Alyssa exclaimed.

"There's family for ya," my dad replied.

Soon after, I broke for some caffeine. I walked to the kitchen, warmed a cup of coffee in the microwave, and smiled when I saw my better half refitting Pop's sheets. She was the one individual (besides the nurses and home health aides) he would allow to arrange his bedding. He wouldn't even let me straighten it.

As I resumed my project, I overheard their conversation grow deeper. Alyssa knew well that their time together was limited, so she had been attempting to learn more about my father since his diagnosis.

"What was your first job?"

"Huh, I washed dishes."

"No way! I can't see you doing that. Where at?"

"The Mermaid in Mounds View."

Upon my partner's prying, Dad obliged her. He described his tour in the Marine Corps, his sandblasting occupation, and the carwash strike he once organized, which got him a raise of twenty-five cents an hour—a decent wage increase in the 1970s. He told her about his gig insulating attics and his eventual thirty-year career in ironworking. Then they remained speechless for several minutes. The only dialogue I caught came from the TV.

Curious, I wandered toward them. It relieved me to discover my pop grabbing some Zs; he'd hardly been sleeping. Not wanting to disturb, I stood in the threshold, quietly observing him deeply breathe in and out. When I shifted to Alyssa, she was napping, too.

I gazed at my lady, who peacefully slumped in her chair. I thought about how fortunate I was to have her. She'd been my source of strength. Not only had she held me while I bawled every night, but she sustained us financially to boot. She actually insisted on picking up extra shifts, so I wouldn't have to work, allowing me to be present for my father. I was grateful for how great she was with my dad as well.

Some people recently admitted to me that they couldn't handle seeing Pop in his frail, emaciated form. Hell, I had to step out to cry on a handful of occasions because he was in obvious agony. But Alyssa never shied away from him. Since she had earned a living at a hospital for years, being around a dying person was nothing new to her. So she had consistently given my father cheerful company, love, and support during the past few months—no matter his mood or condition. I wondered if it was bad for me to be glad she had been "jaded" (the term she regularly used) by her workplace while I returned to my paint tray. She calmly dealt with my old man's disease, which had been a blessing in disguise.

When they woke up, I had been back at my task for about an hour. I concentrated on my second layer, and they picked up where they left off, bashing toothless plaintiffs and deadbeat defendants. I laughed along with their commentary till I wrapped up the final coat around dusk. The front door opened again.

My brother entered the living room as I shuffled out of the bedroom. Comforted that Jay was now there to spend the evening, Alyssa suggested we go home to rest. I didn't resist on account of my exhaustion.

"You always gotta get in that last hug, don't you?" my pop asked.

"Yup!" my squeeze responded while gently squeezing him. "I'll see you this weekend, OK?"

"Sounds like a plan. You know where to find me."

"Bye, Papi."

"Bye, Alyssa. I appreciate all you do."

I assured my father I'd return in the morning and embraced him. We said "I love you" to one another. He called me back, though, right after I turned to leave. He grasped my hand.

"Make sure you're good to her."

"Of course, Dad."

I took his insistence seriously. Alyssa had been nothing but good for the both of us.

20

Anger Mismanagement

From inside our father's 1983 Ford Escort, Jay and I witnessed a man filled with rage. We looked in awe as our dad released his aggression on the coin-operated vacuum at the gas station. Swearing to the skies, he slammed the hose against the ground repeatedly, hoping to clear the obstruction that had prevented the device from removing any dirt from his red hatchback. He continued to punish the apparatus until it finally turned off. Out of cuss words and out of wind, he threw the tube down in disgust. The only thing the cleaner had sucked up was his last quarter.

A quarter-century later, I was the one screaming at a vac.

"What the hell is wrong with this?!"

"The filter probably needs to be cleaned," Pop faintly responded from his hospice bed.

"But Jay just did that the other day!"

I ran the Hoover across the worn living room carpet. Carefully weaving around the bedside tables, which displayed various snacks and meds, I pushed the machine over a handful of cigarette butts that my father had emptied from his ashtray onto the floor next to his wastebasket. It infuriated me to see that the KOOLs survived when I pulled the vacuum back.

"Fuck this!"

I swiftly picked up the appliance and stormed out. I unlocked the front door, kicked opened the screen, and launched it off the steps. The vac loudly crashed upon the snowy lawn. I remained on the cement porch for several minutes.

Although it was early February, I had to cool off. I was sleep-deprived and angry — watching my pop wither away during the past few months had taken a huge toll on me. I gazed at the cloudy, midday sky as I tried to calm down.

After regaining my composure, I wandered into the yard, and lifted the gadget from the snow. I returned to the stoop to test Dad's theory. So I banged the yellow filter against the iron railing till no more dust bunnies sprang out. I reassembled the upright cleaner, took a deep breath, and went inside.

I immediately detected a difference when I plugged it back in. The sweeper sounded much more powerful; I actually heard it inhaling the particles. I promptly got rid of the cigs that had lit my fuse earlier and vacuumed the rest of the area.

"There you go, Pop," I said while unplugging the Hoover. "I don't think the filter was attached correctly."

He grinned at me.

Dad's place in Emerald Hills Village

"What?!"

"Why can't you just admit that I was right?"

"You weren't though! Jay cleaned the fucking filter two days ago!"

He chuckled, and I bolted once again.

I marched to the dining room and stared out the window. The landscape was white, but I only saw red. I was mad at the world, distraught that my father—my best friend—would soon leave me. I couldn't imagine my existence without him. It was clear, because of my recently short temper, that I didn't know how to cope with this harsh reality either. I observed my breath fog up the glass and cried.

"Tyrel!" my dad yelled. "Come in here!"

"Sorry! I'll be right there," I answered, remorseful for my latest tantrum.

I was ashamed of myself. My pop needed love and support, not hissy fits. I hustled back.

When I reentered, he struggled to reach for me with his spindly arm. I hurried to him, holding his right hand with mine.

"I'm sure this is hard on you," he admitted teary-eyed. "And I appreciate all you do."

"I know," I replied, still weeping.

"You've really stepped up to the plate."

"Well, you've taken care of me all my life. You should be at home—this was the least I could..."

His head fell back onto his pillow, and he closed his eyes.

"I love you, Tyrel."

"I love you, too."

His fingers slipped from my grasp, and he slipped into yet another nap.

21

The Red Oak

There's my favorite tree," my dad stated as I parked at the edge of the vacant lot. "Isn't she pretty?"

"Sure is," I answered while staring through the windshield. "So that's the one you've been telling me about."

"Indeed," my old man confirmed. "Well, shall we?"

"I'm ready if you are."

We got out of the Ford and started on a paved trail close by. Mindful of my pace, I ambled alongside my fragile father who now strode gingerly, far slower than the powerful strut he was known for. I noticed he was swimming in his hooded sweatshirt and jeans. It hurt me to see Pop—the guy who I had always viewed as indestructible—was being swallowed by the same clothes his muscles practically used to burst through. I sighed.

Passing a few soccer fields, we neared the tree. It donned rich crimson petals and proudly stood out from its smaller, less striking neighbors. Impressed by its vibrant branches, I stopped twenty yards short of the trunk in order to snap some pics.

"What kind is it?" I inquired from behind my lens.

"A red oak. The leaves turn that cool color this time of year."

"It's beautiful, just like today."

"Yup, but I'm afraid we won't be getting many more like this, sonny boy."

"I suppose; it is already the middle of November," I acknowledged as I

My father's favorite tree

put my camera away. "That blows."

We continued our airing. We spoke about the mild weather, surprised that no one else was in the park on such a pleasant morning. Wandering by several ball fields, we agreed on how much we missed baseball—a subject we had discussed passionately—even though the World Series concluded just a fortnight earlier. Then the conversation suddenly ended. We simply meandered on without saying a word.

We sauntered in awkward silence for a few minutes, and my father turned to me at last.

"Are you gonna be OK when I die?" he asked with a somber face.

I halted abruptly in my tracks. I gazed at the sky while my eyes rapidly welled up. However, this was nothing new. I had done a bunch of crying since his diagnosis in late October. Not only was I losing my pop, but I was losing my best friend, too. And I didn't wish to deal with it.

"I don't know," I finally choked out with tears streaming down my cheeks.

"I worry about you."

Afraid to look at him, I studied the ground for a while. I felt terrible. He had terminal cancer, yet remained concerned about my wellbeing. I lifted my head.

"I don't want you to worry about me, Dad. You have enough on your mind."

"I'll be alright, but I need to know if you're gonna be."

"It's gonna be so hard."

"Tyrel," he added sternly. "You can't let it ruin your life."

"But how?! I don't know what I'm gonna do without you!"

"Life's about tenacity," he replied. "Things will become easier if you hang in there long enough."

After pacing back and forth, I digested what he said and looked him in the eye.

"I'll try my best. I'll get through it … somehow."

"Promise?"

"Promise," I responded with a deep exhale, wiping away my tears.

We resumed our ramble. Changing the subject, we shot the bull the rest of the way. We moseyed by a colorful playground, traipsed past a picnic area, and skirted the southern shore of a reservoir. Our next stop was the pickup.

Upon arrival at the Ranger, my father rested his forearms atop the closed tailgate. The once strapping fellow, who completed three laps around this complex daily, was now winded after one. I quietly stood beside him as he caught his breath.

"Not bad for a dying man," he offered.

"Not bad at all. You did great."

We subsequently scanned Rich Valley Park once more before climbing into the truck.

"Goodbye, tree," Pop uttered in a soft voice while I backed out of our parking spot.

Unfortunately, that would be the final stroll my dad and I would ever take together. The weather worsened dramatically along with his condition. He passed away three months later.

Some weeks after he died, I spent an evening flipping through old pictures, including the ones on my digicam. I instantly wept when I came across the shots of the red oak.

Although it rekindled my sadness, I was glad for this rediscovery. I actually stare at my father's favorite tree a lot these days. The image prompts me to appreciate the small things—the lonely red oaks of the world—something my pop did so well. The picture also brings me back to our last walk and the gorgeous weather we enjoyed that day. But most important, the red oak reminds me of the promise I made to Dad.

22

So Long, Squeak

Every so often, my father devoted a moment to Squeak. He would hold her on his lap, speak to her in a babyish voice, and stroke her smoky fur till she purred.

"I do it to remind her that someone out there still appreciates her," my dad would explain.

Now, Squeak—my pop's high-pitched, polite, yet reticent cat—was on my thigh. And it was our turn to give her some special attention. In fact, my brother and I had dedicated our entire morning to the aged pet.

"We're doing the right thing," I affirmed, trying to convince myself.

I breathed out heavily as the disoriented feline viewed me via the holes of her carrier. I laughed when she tried to stick her charcoal snout through the quarter-sized openings.

"But this really sucks," Jay replied as he concentrated on the snow-lined highway.

"She's miserable, though. We'd be keeping her around for our own selfish reasons."

"Yeah, at least she won't have to suffer anymore. Right, Squeak?"

My younger sibling shifted his peepers from the road to make eye contact with her. She calmly gaped back at him from behind the gate of the small kennel. Almost always well-behaved, she naturally kept cool for the rest of the course.

Fifteen minutes later, the three of us were in a drab room not much bigger than a cubicle. Squeak quietly rested in the cat carrier, which my bro had placed on the countertop, and Jay and I sat on opposite sides of her. We somberly exchanged stories of the fragile feline until a girl came in. She opened the holder, and Squeak rigidly crept out, curiously sniffing the unfamiliar air around her. Long strands of drool hung from her chin.

"It says here that her first visit was March 1994," the employee stated while scrolling through the patient history on a computer in the corner. "So, besides being old, what's wrong with her?"

"She's rickety, her hearing is shot, and she can't see anything remotely close to her," I answered. "Plus, I'm not sure if it started with a tooth infection, but her jaw is in awful shape."

"Oh gosh," the veterinarian realized as she inspected the gaping, bloody wound that had eroded most of Squeak's left cheek.

"She can hardly eat anymore," my brother added. "We've just been able to feed her soft stuff for the past few months."

The vet informed Jay and me of what would happen next. However, I barely heard her; Squeak memories distracted me. Clear recollections, like how she would unfailingly chirp back at me whenever I called out her name, were weighing my heart down.

I dreaded the immediate future and retired to my seat against the wall. I watched my sib pat Squeak's matted fur while he and the woman discussed the payment. He handed over his credit card.

"Take as much time as you need," the lady offered. She slipped my bro's plastic to him. "Knock when you're ready."

We took turns petting Squeak over the ensuing minutes. She stood in place and closed her eyes, thoroughly enjoying our affection. She let out the shrill meows she had been named after nearly two decades ago. Both of us misty-eyed, Jay and I assured her she would be OK.

"Well, let's not drag this out anymore than we have to," I finally suggested.

My brother nodded, spun around, and rapped on the door. A girl sporting a ponytail appeared, scooped up the oblivious feline, and left the ashen room.

Our mouser was returned shortly thereafter. Her right front leg was wrapped, equipped with a catheter. Although she relaxed, Jay and I resumed stroking the cat in order to comfort her to the fullest. Next, a young woman donning scrubs walked in and introduced herself. She joined us in caressing Squeak as she described the looming procedure.

"Is she going to feel anything?" I asked.

"No, she'll basically be getting an overdose of anesthesia," the brunette doctor responded. "It'll be painless."

"Will it take long?" my kin questioned.

"Nope, it goes pretty fast."

Jay and I reluctantly gave the green light, figuring it wouldn't serve any good to delay things further.

The gal inserted the syringe into the catheter and slowly pressed down. Squeak leaned forward, and my brother ran his hand across her back repeatedly. I scratched her head, telling her she'd be in a better place while tears trickled down my face. She glanced at me and stared at the countertop. She noiselessly collapsed onto her left side as the liquid drained to the barrel's halfway point. Uncertain if she was still alive, I continued to pet Squeak to avoid the possibility of her feeling alone for even a millisecond. I could see she no longer saw from her copper eyes. When the plunger was all the way down, I peeked up to discover that Jay wept, too.

"She's gone," the doc announced after checking Squeak's limp body in a few different spots with her stethoscope. "I'm so sorry."

"She was around for a long time," I choked out. "We have a lot of memories with her."

"Do you guys need more time with her?"

"No, thank you," I replied. "We've already said our goodbyes." I held the exit open for my bro.

I was sobbing. Sensing the gawks of a lobby full of staff and clientele, I tailed J as we hustled out of the animal hospital. I was distraught—I couldn't lock eyes with anyone, nor did I wish that anybody look at me. I had to escape that building ASAP.

Once outside, we bolted for the red Honda Accord. Without saying a word, we climbed into the car and slammed the doors. Jay stomped on the gas, fleeing the parking lot as quickly as he could.

The ride began in silence. Even though we knew it would be difficult, watching Squeak depart was far harder than we had expected. Her passing crushed our already fragile states of mind.

We were severely wounded by the death of our parent, which had occurred nine days earlier; the funeral four after that. In the meantime, we had been emptying our dad's trailer and were comforted to see Squeak waiting for us whenever we entered. Despite her declining health, not only did she bring some needed life to those desolate rooms—the forlorn place where our pop died—but she also represented something that our father truly cared about. She was a link to our dad, and now that connection was severed as well. And so was another piece of the world we used to recognize.

"I've about had it, Jay" I eventually admitted, gazing out the passenger window.

"I know; too much death for me," he acknowledged with his sunglasses fixed on his lane.

"Poor Squeak. I never want to do that again."

"Me neither."

"Pop was right—you get attached to the fuckers."

I turned back to the wintry landscape. To block out what we had just witnessed, I chose not to reflect on Squeak as she was near the end: decrepit and dirty. Instead, I preferred to concentrate on the cute, plump cat with the healthy gray coat I had known for over half my existence. I remembered the occasion my bro and I tended to her while she gave birth to a litter of five in the living room. I smiled upon recalling the countless occasions I would find her sleeping in a cabinet, atop a heat register, or underneath a chair. This reminded me of the humorous poems my father had written over the years to depict her habits. I had actually discovered many Squeak rhymes that my dad had scribbled on random scraps when I recently sifted through his piles of paperwork. And thinking of my pop led me to more sadness. I remained pensive for the duration of the drive.

It was noon when we pulled up behind my truck. I scanned the lonely double-wide, took a deep breath, and reached for the handle. Noticing my brother was about to turn off his idling vehicle, I stopped him.

"Go home, Jay," I insisted. "We can clean some more tomorrow."

He agreed. We had had enough for one day.

23

Matted Down

Are these all lawn chemicals, sir?"

"Fuck!" I yelled.

The tall employee jumped backward. He nervously put his paws in the pockets of his navy jumpsuit.

"I mean … yeah. Sorry about that," I stated. "Here you go, man."

He collected two homer buckets from me filled to the brim with pesticides and leaky fertilizer containers, which I had recently discovered in a garbage container my pop hid behind his abode ages ago. The worker jerked his head back upon catching a whiff of the waste.

"Now all you need to do is run inside so they can scan your driver's license."

But I already knew that—this kid had actually helped me on umpteen visits during the past month. I nonetheless kept my mouth closed. I couldn't expect him to remember my mug amid the countless faces he saw every shift.

"OK, thank you."

"You're welcome, sir. Have a nice day."

I slammed the Ranger's tailgate shut, shaking my noggin in frustration at the streams of bright green liquid slowly creeping across my pickup bed. The overpowering stench that had pursued me from my dad's wouldn't be so easy to shake after all. I decided that my next stop would have to be the carwash. Satisfied with my plan, I went inside.

I approached the old guy at the counter—the same friendly gent who was always there. He immediately recognized me, too. We exchanged nods.

"So, what was it today?" he asked. He scanned my ID and hit a button on his dusty keyboard.

"Just hazardous liquids," I answered as he handed over my identification.

"Well, that's free," he affirmed. "You should buy some cookies with the money you saved."

I followed his eyes to spot a couple of Girl Scouts seated at a plastic folding table.

I chuckled as I turned back to the attendant, aware that my drop-off wouldn't have cost me a dime, anyway. And by his smirk, he knew that I knew.

"I'll take a look."

"Thanks," he replied with a smile.

I left the recycling center with a box of thin mints in hand and a carwash on my mind.

I sped to a service station a mile down the road. While I hauled along the highway, it annoyed me to catch my gas gage on E. Despite my strong desire to immediately beeline for the carwash and eliminate the fumes that had been burning my nostrils all morning, I advanced to one of the pumps instead.

I had to act fast. Not only did my knees nearly buckle for the foul odor coming from the bed, but my windbreaker was also inadequate for the fifteen-degree air. Holding my breath, I swiped my check card, removed the gas cap, shoved in the fuel dispenser, pressed down the silver clip to sustain pressure on the spout, and hustled back into the auto.

I wasn't in the cab long when I detected that the handle flicked off. I checked the needle and saw that it stopped at 75 percent full. So I climbed out and pushed down the metal fastener, but the attachment clicked off after just a few ticks. I attempted again to no avail. I even squeezed the grip with my freezing hands, but no luck. With the funk from my pickup bed getting stronger and my patience becoming shorter, I ultimately accepted that I was leaving with three-fourths of a tank. I hammered the nozzle back on the pump, snatched my receipt, and raced the Ford toward the carwash.

Within a couple of minutes, I was in a dark tunnel, surrounded by powerful sprayers and enormous brushes. Surprisingly, there were no cars ahead of me—I couldn't recall the last moment I didn't have to hang in a line. Despite my rough start, things were perhaps evening out for me. Through the windshield, I joyfully watched while machinery pre-soaked, washed, rinsed, and waxed my ride, finally ridding it of the nasty substances. I happily drove forward when the buzzer for the blower sounded. I'd be en route to my house shortly.

Nevertheless, as the machine's ninety-second cycle was winding down, I perceived in my rearview that the rubber mat in the tail of my truck was violently flapping. I had noticed this before, though, and continued to inch along in order to maximize the dryer. All was fine till the blower took a mighty last gasp, causing the protector to leap out of the bed. I sat in shock while it slid back into the belly of the beast.

I jumped out of the Ranger and hurried to the stall, attempting to rescue the mat before the next car arrived. But I only scurried a few steps. The woman behind me squinted at the covering through her windshield, established eye contact with me, and moved ahead anyhow. I threw my fists up in disbelief when the asshole rested the leading passenger wheel of her silver Civic on my coverture. I furiously climbed back into my pickup, whipped around to the side of the carwash, and waited to try again when she finished.

The instant the Honda left, however, a vehicle drove in, then an additional one after that, and another, and so on. In hopes that I'd eventually have my shot, I loitered outside checking the PSI in my tires, adjusting my mirrors, and simply sitting in the Ford to keep warm from the early March temperature. But the train of autos appeared to grow longer each time I peeked around the corner. I reluctantly swallowed my pride and entered the building.

"I can't do anything about it right now," the middle-aged woman explained while observing a black-and-white monitor behind the counter. "A car is in there."

"Could you shut it down for a few seconds when this wash is over?"

"Nope. The only way is to wait until it's not being used."

"There's a bunch of cars out there!"

"That's what happens on a sunny Saturday."

"Awesome. I'm going to be here ALL DAY!"

I sensed that her fellow cashier, not to mention the half dozen customers in her line, was staring at me.

"Well, let me see," the manager offered.

She vanished behind the swinging "Employees Only" gate.

Several minutes wore on, and the raspy-voiced blonde reappeared. She grinned as she waved me toward her. I couldn't help but notice that her khakis and winter boots were dripping wet.

I trailed her to a small entryway in the rear and glanced at the floor to discover that the access was being propped open by the pad—one half in the corridor, the other in the carwash. She got it! And, by her expression, she was through with it.

I grabbed the covering with both hands and instantly realized it was leaden. The added water weight made it almost impossible to carry. I figured I couldn't leave through the occupied carwash, so I looked around for another exit.

"How should I get this out of here?"

"Through the front of the store."

"Of course," I uttered with a sigh. "I've probably been through this carwash fifty times over the years, and this has never happened. Have you ever seen anything like this?"

"Never."

"I'm really sorry you had to do this. Thank you."

"Oh, you're welcome," she responded prior to disappearing into an office.

Upon dragging the mat completely into the hallway, I struggled to stand it upright. I tightly coiled the covering and wrapped my arms around it. To burst through the swinging door, I led with my back and returned to the center of the floor. I tried my best to ignore the endless glares, whispers, and giggles while I slothfully lumbered like a penguin, bear hugging the roll until I exited.

Filthy, freezing, soaking, and exhausted, I mustered enough strength to throw the covering into the truck. I fired up the motor and floored it.

I pondered what had just occurred as I angrily tore down the interstate. It all seemed unreal; I was about to blow a gasket. I needed to talk to someone, and there was one person who came to mind.

A half hour later, I was dashing atop drifts at Fort Snelling National Cemetery. Over the uneven, snowy terrain, I stumbled by countless markers before I reached him. I hunched for a minute, panting over my father's brilliant white, newly chiseled headstone. The floral arrangement from his funeral—now brittle and brown—still adorned his grave. This was a sad reminder that only three weeks had passed since the Memorial Rifle Squad discharged three volleys in his honor.

After I caught my wind, I told my pop of the day's events. I practically heard him laughing while I described my disastrous morning. I imagined him sharing an embarrassing story of his own just to make me feel better—something he had done on various occasions. Although he said nothing back, I knew he was listening.

I stood in silence. Thinking about how much I missed my dad, I stayed till shivers got the best of me. I patted the top of his marker and assured him that I'd return soon.

I drove a little slower on the way home.

24

Megan and Andra

I was a lucky dude to be in a booth with a trinity of beautiful brunettes. Alyssa was always at my side, and the two women facing me had been there for me almost as often. I actually met them during the fall before Alyssa danced into my life. While my girlfriend entertained the gals by singing Celine Dion into her butter knife, I shook my head recalling the awkwardness of the first time Andra, Megan, and I ever spoke; or failed to speak, that is.

Flashing on a year and a half earlier, Megan and Andra sit across from me again. But we are in a conference room, not a pub. Upon the prompt of our new bosses, we reluctantly present ourselves. One by one, we all finish in thirty seconds. Perhaps it is nerves, or maybe we are all having a bad day, but we continue to keep our remarks to a minimum. I would find out later that our supervisors genuinely worried if the three of us would get along based on the lack of chat at our introduction. However, we would soon ease any uneasiness regarding our initial poor rapport.

The ladies and I next converged in Indianapolis for our VISTA training. The four-day weekend comprised monotonous workshops. With two dozen fellow group members, we dissected destitution repeatedly by staring at endless overheads and tossing a ball around to force each attendee to rehash the topic. (Whoever caught the pill had to opine.) Although we cared deeply about poverty in America, Andra, Megan, and I were sick of beating a dead horse. Drawn together by our burnout, we carried through the wearisome sessions over crossword puzzles, hotel buffets, and coffee breaks. We spent our nights on the town too, exerting pent-up energy and getting to know one another. We discovered that we were all open-minded, well-traveled, driven to do some good in the world, and shared a deep appreciation for sarcasm to boot. So we hit it off after all. And our trio would remain tight far beyond our orientation in the Hoosier State.

Throughout the following thirteen months, our colleagues (who started their service year twelve weeks before us) basically viewed Megan, Andra, and me as one. We invariably arrived to and departed from our Friday meetings jointly. If we weren't together, our cohorts would ask why. And if our triumvirate separated, it wasn't my choice. Not only did I prefer to be around my pals, but it also came to be that I would need them … more than they could have ever expected.

My buds stepped up while plenty of others disappeared after my father's diagnosis. They refused to avoid me just because they were unsure how to act toward me. For example, they talked to me at our holiday party — our last afternoon on the job — when the remaining seventeen VISTAs clearly steered clear of me. They expressed their concern directly instead of through other people. (Whatshisname "asked about you" or whatshername "says they're sorry about your dad," I'd hear now and then from Andra, Megan, or Alyssa.) They weren't available only when it proved convenient for them. They didn't take days on end to reply to my messages or pencil me in for a half hour on a weeknight. Nor did they arrange far off plans with me, which fell by the wayside as the meeting date drew close.

Instead, they reached out to me. They consistently emailed me words of encouragement. They lured me out of my or my old man's house every week for coffee as well. And they simply listened at our gatherings, providing me with much-needed ears, besides Alyssa's, to which I could let out the emotions I had bottled up since I had seen them last. Except for my dear high school bud of fifteen years, Megan and Andra were the two friends I counted on for support when my pop was dying. Naturally, they hugged me at his funeral. And they've continued to be supportive.

In fact, the girls, along with Alyssa's constant urging, were the reason I had left the unintimidating confines of home on this rare occasion; I just felt comfortable around them. Our dinner at this bar was the first instance in practically a month I had socialized.

"What's the title of your book going to be?" Megan asked me when Alyssa had finished her ballad.

"Megan and Andra!" Andra immediately chimed in.

My answer wouldn't echo hers, but I had a couple of solid reasons.

Our story isn't over yet. I owe a lot to them — they're important to me. So

I sincerely hope they stay a part of my circle years down the road.

Plus, no narrative, never mind a paperback, would be long enough for me to convey my gratitude for Andra and Megan's friendship.

25

Treading Water

One of my earliest memories still gives me chills. I am four. It is a sunny summer afternoon. I am on a small boat in the middle of a lake, watching my father and his older brother, Milo, cast their fishing lines. My dad asks me to grab him a minnow.

Eager to help, I scurry to the edge of the aluminum craft. I lean over. I stretch toward the yellow bait bucket floating in the H20 below. However, the container's plastic push-in door is slightly beyond my reach. No matter which arm I use, or how I contort myself, I merely graze the opening with my fingertips. I am determined to come through for Pop, though. So I lunge with all my might.

SPLASH! I am suddenly in the drink. I don't know how to swim. Nor does it bother me. Too young to comprehend the urgency of the situation, I can only study my murky surroundings while I sink.

But I hear a distant plunge. Following the abrupt squeeze of an arm wrapped around my torso, the liquid gets brighter as I am propelled to the surface like a rocket. I read the relief written across my uncle's face while I bob in my father's embrace.

Recollections such as the aforementioned have kept me up at night throughout the eight weeks after Dad's passing. I reflect upon the many occasions — beginning with my unplanned dive and onward through the twenty-seven years to come — on which he took care of me. I cry when I think about the countless phone calls, nature walks, and talks over breakfast during which he offered me counsel. And I am especially saddened when I realize how we can no longer do those things.

To be honest, I've been that four-year-old in the water ever since he died. I am much like the boy who couldn't swim; to navigate the world without him has been quite challenging. I constantly battle depression, have insomnia, and can't concentrate on squat outside of my writing. So I keep grasping for my pop, hoping he'll jump in and save me from the depths in which I find myself on most days. I visit his grave, speak to him when I'm alone, and regularly look at the pictures of him displayed around my office. Usually, I focus on a particular photo of me when I was a toddler.

I am one. It appears like we're dressed for a Sunday. I am sitting on my father's knee in the middle of my childhood living room, watching the camera with him. I can gather from his smile that he is happy to show off his son. He would maintain that expression for the next three decades, consistently informing others of his content. More important, he would tell me; even as he neared the end.

My dad was actually more worried about me than himself when he was dying. I spent each day with him during his final four months, and he could see that his impending death devastated me. He knew he was my best friend, and he recognized that I was losing my mind as I constantly stayed busy by doing chores, inventing home improvement projects, or simply pacing around his house. As a result, he made me sit down every so often to put me at ease. He would call me to his bedside to say that he loved me and state that I had always done him proud. These moments meant a lot to me because the last thing I ever wanted was to disappoint him. I never plan on disappointing him.

For that reason, I wish to lead my life in a way that would honor him. I hope to accomplish this by keying in on what he did so effortlessly: stay true to myself and others, be humble, and not take anything for granted. This, too, will be a manner for my father to live through me. And when I wander off my path, I shall seek his guidance; another avenue for me to keep him alive. I'll surely be mindful of his past advice as well.

In fact, I have a note of his posted above my desk.

Ease up on yourself and appreciate those who love you!

Love,

Dad

I have tried to heed this suggestion from the morning he wrote it to me almost a decade ago. I will strive to regard it from now on. Pop's never led me astray, and I'm certain if I continue to reach out to him during this tough time — by far the hardest I've endured — I'll be back in the boat once again.

Mom, Dad, and me in 1980

Notes

Not a Plain Jay

Nelson, Tyrel. "Not a 'Plain Jay'." *The Ironworker*, Jul. 2003, pp. 19-20.

Chapter One: Bass Ponds

Nelson, Tyrel. "Bass Ponds." Hackwriters, Aug. 2009, http://www.hackwriters.com/bassponds.htm.

Chapter Two: The Power of Ten

Nelson, Tyrel. "Local team builds in Mexico." Twin Cities Habitat for Humanity, 29 Sep. 2012, https://www.tchabitat.org/blog/local-team-builds-in-mexico.

Nelson, Tyrel. "The Power of Ten – Habitat for Humanity in Puerto Angel, Mexico." BootsnAll, https://www.bootsnall.com/articles/the-power-of-ten.html.

Nelson, Tyrel. "The Power of Ten: Volunteering in Oaxaca." inTravel Magazine, 3 Jul. 2009, https://www.intravelmag.com/intravel/involved/the-power-of-ten-volunteering-in-oaxaca.

Chapter Four: Amanda and the Arboretum

Nelson, Tyrel. "Amanda and the Arboretum." Hackwriters, 16 Nov. 2009, http://www.hackwriters.com/Arboretum.htm.

Chapter Five: The Cemetery and Me

Nelson, Tyrel. "The Cemetery and Me." Hackwriters, Dec. 2009, http://www.hackwriters.com/cemeteryTN.htm.

Chapter Six: The Other Tyrel

Nelson, Tyrel. "The Other Tyrel." Hackwriters, Jan. 2010, http://www.hackwriters.com/Tyrel09.htm.

Chapter Nine: A Bowl of Fruit

Nelson, Tyrel. "A Bowl Of Fruit." The Expeditioner, 7 Apr. 2010, http://www.theexpeditioner.com/2010/04/07/a-bowl-of-fruit/#more-6385.

Chapter Ten: An Afternoon in Antigua

Nelson, Tyrel. "An Afternoon in Antigua." Hackwriters, Mar. 2010, https://www.hackwriters.com/AntiguaTN.htm.

Chapter Twelve: On Call

Abbott Northwestern Hospital: https://www.allinahealth.org/abbott northwestern-hospital.

Angioplasty: http://dictionary.reference.com/browse/angioplasty.

Cardiovascular Technologist: https://www.yourfreecareertest.com/cardiovascular-technologist/.

Interventional Cardiologist:
https://www.youtube.com/watch?v=JF1DsgO_KlY.

Radiologic and MRI Technologists:
https://www.bls.gov/ooh/healthcare/radiologic-technologists.htm.

Registered Nurses: https://www.bls.gov/ooh/healthcare/registered-nurses.htm.

Stent: http://dictionary.reference.com/browse/stent.

Other Works by Tyrel Nelson

Stories from Ecuador: A Collection by Tyrel Nelson

Stories from Ecuador is a collection of honest, first-hand accounts of the most memorable people, places, and moments from a young man's year-long journey in Latin America. Tyrel Nelson's prose breathes life into the characters he  befriends along the way and sketches scenes with the telescopic perspective that one only gains by stepping outside the American mainstream. Setting off from Quito to begin his training to teach English (TESOL), you tag along traversing the Ecuadorian countryside surrounding Cuenca as Nelson documents his experiences and transformation from a Minnesota native into a true citizen of the world. Using the rich landscape as the backdrop for his stories, he not only shows a keen eye for cultural and historical detail, but an artist's flare for blending personal perspective with the attributes of a solid narrative. From the encounters with his quirky landlord and neighbors in Cuenca to quixotic adventures with his brother, Nelson serves up a colorful mix of tales incorporating levity, beauty and even boredom, in an unexpected and refreshing way. — Daniel Patrick Holmay

Travels and Tribulations

In his latest book of short stories, Tyrel Nelson immerses you in his peripatetic world, transporting you to old haunts and sharing his latest meditations.  Through Tyrel's personal and spiritual meanderings you become fully invested in people from all walks of life. You appreciate Doña Vicky treating you like family, imagining her sending an unmentioned smile your way. You seek escape in a sweaty adventure with eager explorers wanting to lend a helping hand. You sit by his mother's bedside each day, as she grows weaker. These stories build upon each other and draw you into transformative relationships that linger — from bittersweet moments of tearful overseas goodbyes to heartbreaking devastation at the loss of two parents. With intimate simplicity and a playful tone, the writing style invites you to observe the narrator gradually coming to terms with regret and loss but ultimately finding inspiration and meaning in both his past and present. — Andra Bosneag

Made in the USA
Monee, IL
27 December 2021

ba5c979e-19f2-434f-839a-500e123f18dfR01